To Jim Effert —
an entrepreneur in education!
— a man of vision!

Best Regards
John Pierson
8/15/93

WIN SOME, LOSE SOME

WIN SOME, LOSE SOME

My 40 Years in Corporate America

John V. Titsworth, Hon.D.Eng.

The Information Economics Press

New Canaan, Connecticut

WIN SOME, LOSE SOME:
MY 40 YEARS IN CORPORATE AMERICA
The Information Economics Press / April 1992
Limited Edition

"John Titsworth, From Farm Boy to Chairman"
Printed by permission of Ingram Micro Inc., Santa Ana, California

Library of Congress Catalog Card No. 91-76795

ISBN 0-962-04133-5

Printed in the United States of America

*In memory of my parents, who taught me
the value and comfort of fair play and honesty.*

CONTENTS

ACKNOWLEDGMENTS

For years I have enjoyed telling "Bill Lear" stories. People who would listen to these and other anecdotes about my business career would often say, "John, you should write a book!"

So, here it is.

Thanks go to all of my family and friends who encouraged me to go ahead with this endeavor, including Vera Dolan, my editor and consultant, whose diligence and timely advice have been invaluable.

I warmly thank my four children, John, Steven, Susan, and Sandra, for being the best kids anyone could have. They have not only helped make my success easier, but also a lot of fun.

Especially above all, I thank my wife, Jeanette, who stood by me in the good and bad times.

AN OPENING WORD

I would hope that this story of a farm boy who grows up to be Executive Vice President of one of the largest companies in the U.S., and then to Chairman of the Board of one of the most prestigious colleges in America will encourage young people who aspire to a successful career.

I hope this book will help them understand that one doesn't achieve success without winning part of the time *and* without losing part of the time. One doesn't accomplish much without trying. If you don't work hard and take risks, you may not lose but you will *never* win.

I like to tell young people that education is the key to real success. It is a "ticket to the game." Without an education, you can't play in the game and won't even get to watch.

The other thing which I like to remind young people is that one doesn't need to set lofty goals. Hard work, honesty, and fair play will create opportunities that lead to a successful career.

I

THE FARM BOY

Most people today were not around during the Depression years or are too young to remember much about them. Those who do remember, and those who have had those years described to them, think of it as a trying, if not terrible, period.

My family was certainly affected economically by the Great Depression, but my memories of the 1930s are far from depressed—indeed, they are some of my fondest memories.

I was born in 1925 in the small town of Hutsonville, Illinois. Doctors made housecalls in those days and they delivered babies at home. Such was the case with me—in a rented house located on Hutson Creek where it enters the Wabash River.

My Dad's name was Walter Valentine Titsworth, and he was known as "Val" by everyone. My Mom's name was Mabel Poorman Titsworth.

Dad was a barber and a good one, but was not in that profession by choice. His father, Joshua Titsworth, had died in 1924 and my father's older brother, Uncle Chalon, had inherited the family home and farm. As a result, Dad got sent to barber school in Indianapolis!

I can remember the house in Hutsonville, even though we left there when I was only four. I remember the screened back porch and specifically, I remember helping Dad gather the fishing poles and digging for worms so we could go fishing in Hutson Creek. You could catch bluegills, bass, and catfish in Hutson Creek. Dad was a good cane pole-and-bobber fisherman.

In the Wabash River, you could catch channel cats, carp, and buffalo, but these were caught by commercial fishermen with seines and trot lines. We ate a lot of carp; it is pretty good when it is deep fried and if you watch for the bones.

A barber who didn't own a shop could make 15 cents per haircut in 1929. The going price was 25 cents, but the shopowner got 10 cents. At that rate, Dad couldn't make a living and support a wife and two kids (my brother Tom was born in 1927).

Although the family home had gone to Uncle Chalon, my grandmother, Elizabeth Titsworth, had retained 60 acres which she decided to let my Dad farm, rent free. In 1929, she also built us a house.

I can remember visiting the site of our new home on the dirt road a mile south of Trimble, Illinois, a town of about 100 people. The construction had just started, and I clearly recall seeing the bright orange-colored studs sticking up from the poured cement basement. At four years of age, I don't recall thinking of how elegant a brand new house would be, but I do remember how happy and proud Mom was.

The two bedrooms, living room, dining room, and kitchen all together were 850 square feet, plus a full basement. Although the house seemed comfortable enough, there were some features missing. There was no electricity, no indoor toilet, and no running water. We had a three-hole outhouse located about 200 feet from the back door.

There was a cistern that caught water runoff from the roof which provided water for washing clothes and baths, but the water was not fit for drinking. Drinking water came from a pump in the barnlot. It was carried in a bucket to the kitchen each day, except when the well ran dry in the summer. Then, it was carried from a neighbor's well located a half mile down the dirt road, usually by Mom.

A pump in the kitchen brought in the rain water from the cistern, which also went dry in summer. That's when the pump would bring up a few toads and worms from the mud and silt that had collected on the bottom of the cistern.

Until I was about ten years old, my brother Tom and I were washed with a rag from a pan of water every morning. Mom would stand us up on the counter stark naked and scrub away. We were the cleanest kids in the Trimble School, without a doubt. This included our faded clothes and the new shoes we got every fall when school started.

Our shoes, which were usually high-tops, had to last until April, when school was out for the summer. After then, there were no more shoes until fall. That suited Tom and me just fine, because going barefoot gave a feeling of freedom I haven't enjoyed since.

Our new house did have some nice things, like a coal furnace. There were two registers, one large one in the center of the house and one in the bathroom. However, the bathroom wasn't used because it didn't have plumbing.

Mom also had a wood-burning cook stove in the kitchen. With the large register in the archway between the living room and dining room, plus the cook stove, the house stayed warm in the winter. It didn't matter that there was no heat in the bedrooms, we would just use more covers on our beds.

In the summer, the temperature can climb to 100 degrees in southern Illinois, yet the wood cook stove was used morning, noon, and night. Sometimes it may have been 120 degrees in the kitchen, but Mom whistled and sang away. She fixed the best meals I ever had, along with cakes, pies, and cookies baked in an uncontrolled oven.

You haven't lived until you've had biscuits, gravy, and fried quail for breakfast.

There were a lot of quail in the 1930s and 1940s in Illinois. The quail hunting season from November 10 to December 10 was something for which my Dad and Uncle Chalon could hardly wait. They were both crack shots. They were always law-abiding citizens, except when it came to possession limits. During hunting season, the daily limit was 15 birds and the possession limit was 30.

But how could you hunt every day and get 15 birds every day and stay within the possession limit? We ate them almost as fast as Dad got them. We couldn't freeze them, as there was no refrigerator. In November it wasn't cold enough outside to freeze anything.

So, we had quail for breakfast, quail in the lunch pail at school, and quail for supper. We never got tired of it and were sorry when the season ended.

The 1930s were great times for those in the countryside who had enough to eat. We didn't know we were poor.

Everything centered around the family, which included my aunts, uncles, cousins, and my two grandmothers.

I never knew my grandfathers. Both died before I was born.

My Mom's father, Thomas Poorman, was a successful farmer from West Union, Illinois. There, his father, my great-grandfather, had owned half the town, the flour mill, and a great deal of land. My grandfather had inherited one of the farms.

In 1910, Grandfather Poorman had one of the first Ford automobiles in the area. Unfortunately, he had flipped the car over and broke a rib, which punctured his lung. He didn't go to the hospital immediately, thinking he was only bruised. By the time he eventually got there, it was too late. He had made history in Clark County by being one of the first auto fatalities, at age 43.

Grandmother Gertrude Poorman, three teenaged uncles, my Mom and Aunt Mary managed to hold on to the farm and even prosper a bit. Several years before I was born, my grandmother was convinced by a local lawyer to buy the adjacent farm, using her free and clear land and house as collateral.

You can guess what happened. My widowed grandmother and five kids couldn't make one of the payments on the new farm during a poor crop year, so she lost the new place and the old place, including the house. The bank got the new place and somehow the lawyer got the old place. From that time until Grandmother Poorman died in 1960, she rented houses up and down Illinois Route 1, sometimes for several years and sometimes for only a few months.

My other grandmother, Grandmother Titsworth, was also a widow. My Grandfather Titsworth had died of pneumonia in 1924. One cold winter night, he had run about a mile across the fields to a neighbor's burning house to be sure no one was trapped inside. He had been suffering from a bad chest cold, and hadn't bothered to put on more than a robe in his haste to warn the neighbors of the fire. In those days, if you got pneumonia, your chances of recovery were not good. A few days later, he died.

My brother and I loved to visit our grandmothers' places.

Grandmother Poorman always rented a house on a farm, so we had a ball playing in the barns and romping through the house. Grandmother Poorman was a big, strong, frontier woman and very tolerant of little boys. She was uneducated, but was intelligent and outgoing. Perhaps being raised with six brothers and the Irish name Cork gave her an attitude of command and assurance. We knew she was bossy, but we also knew she was tolerant and kind.

Grandmother Titsworth was a very sophisticated college-educated lady. She was small, bent-over and quiet, and wore very thick glasses. She was so nearsighted that she hadn't known what trees or flowers looked like until her parents discovered her problem when she was about ten years old.

Although she never could see all that well, she had the best flower garden in town at her home in Robinson. She had built a new house when Grandfather Titsworth died. She also was an artist and painted several oils of wildlife and still life.

Whenever we visited Grandmother Titsworth's house, it was a quiet time. When I was in my teens and going to Robinson High School, I would stop by her house after school and we would play anagrams for hours—a pretty sedate game.

I thought highly of both my grandmothers, but they were as different as two people could be. We would never think of staying overnight at Grandmother Titsworth's house, and never did. To this day, I'm not sure why. On the other hand, we were always staying overnight at Grandmother Poorman's.

Grandmother Titsworth always treated Mom very well, but I had the feeling that she just didn't quite approve. For some reason, it seems Dad and Mom were treated just a little bit "second class." Dad always got along with his brother, Uncle Chalon, but he was really more of a buddy to my Mom's brothers, my Uncles John, Joe, and Harold.

The Trimble grade school was one mile north of our farm in the town of Trimble. The school had two rooms, the "big" room and the "little" room. Actually, the rooms were the same physical size, but little people went to the "little" room (grades 1 through 4) and big kids went to the "big" room (grades 5 through 8).

It usually took me a long time to get to grade school in Trimble, even though it was only a mile away. It shouldn't take long to walk a mile to school, but there were lots of things to see and do.

The first half mile of dirt road had tall hedges growing on both sides. These nearly made a canopy over the road. Every kind of bird lived in those hedges: blue jays, cardinals, flickers, red-winged blackbirds, catbirds, purple grackles, sparrows, titmice, owls, hawks, doves and, of course, quail. I knew every bird by his song and manner of flight. It took a long time to walk that half mile because I looked at every bird I could find.

It was also fun to kick hedge apples or throw heavy clods at the ones still on the trees. Hedge apples look like large green grapefruit with warts. They were the inedible fruit of the hedge tree.

The last half mile went pretty fast because it was wide open prairie. In winter, with the temperature near zero degrees and the wind at 20 miles per hour, the wind chill must have been 50 degrees below zero. We moved quickly on that last half mile!

Miss Belva Correll was my first and second grade teacher and also my seventh and eighth grade teacher. She was the world's greatest teacher! In the seventh and eighth grades, I never missed a word on the daily spelling tests. This did not occur because I was reasonably bright, but because Miss Belva expected it of me.

My grade school days were not always pleasant. My fourth grade teacher, whose name I won't mention, once called my parents to the school for a conference. She explained that they should not look forward to a very successful academic future for me; certainly, I would never qualify for high school.

The fact was, she said, that I was just not very bright. In particular, I was dull and not interested in what she was teaching. My parents didn't seem to be too concerned, as I recall. My Mom thought the teacher was just plain wrong, and I don't think Dad gave a damn about what the teacher thought.

The problem was that I already knew everything the teacher was trying to teach me, so why pay any attention to her? My Mom's proudest day was when I recently received an honorary doctorate from my college, and was made Citizen of the Year in Robinson, with a banquet for 500 people. My fourth grade teacher was in the audience—46 years later.

I was often sick when I was small. I think I had just about every disease you could get and some the local family doctor didn't understand. I even had my tonsils out twice!

There was a doctor in another town who was cheaper than the good doctor in Robinson. Besides being cheaper, it turned out he was drunk most of the time, including the day he tried to remove my tonsils. He apparently got part of one and managed to cut some things he shouldn't have, such as my uvula, that little bell-shaped thing that hung down the center of my throat. I think I was five when that happened.

A couple of years later, the operation was performed correctly by another doctor.

The year I had my first tonsil operation, I also developed a growth on the side of my neck. It kept getting bigger and bigger, until it was the size of a softball and started to cut off my breathing. In my family, we didn't go to the doctor unless it was absolutely necessary. However, because I couldn't breathe, we went.

The doctor lanced this awful thing, without anesthetic. It eventually grew smaller and disappeared. About 50 years later, during a routine physical exam, a young intern asked me what the scar on my neck was. When I explained, he looked puzzled and asked me if I had ever drunk raw milk as a kid. I said, "Of course, didn't everyone?" He said I didn't have a simple infected gland, but more likely I had tuberculosis!

I had other unpleasant medical problems, not counting the times my younger brother Tom would beat up on me or knock me cold with a brickbat. I could be running full speed and he could still hit me in the head with a rock or part of a brick. He maintains that he learned "lead" in those days by practicing on me. Maybe that is why he is such a good wing shot today.

I suffered from severe hay fever. I'd get it during the wheat threshing season so badly that I could do nothing else but lay flat on my back, gasping for breath, for most of the month of July. When I got older, it didn't improve but I managed to get around. During those times, I wore a mask, although it did very little good. Somehow, wheezing and coughing, I was able to work in the fields.

Farming 60 acres during the Depression was a tough life for a man. We kids worked hard also, but we never felt the pressing responsibilities. I must say, though, that it never seemed to bother Dad much—that is, the responsibility. Nevertheless, he worked harder than any man should have.

Dad was a grain farmer, which meant that he never raised cattle or dairy cows. In fact, he hated them.

We had one cow which provided milk for the family. My brother and I sometimes did the milking in the evening when we were old enough. We would carry the milk to the house and strain it through a cloth. This did a pretty good job of removing the straw and cow manure, which invariably got in the bucket when the cow swished her tail. The milk was kept in the ice box and drunk raw or used in cooking. We would also churn butter about once a week.

Dad had two teams of draft animals on the farm—a team of mules named Jack and Jerry, and a pair of horses. The mules were by far the best workers. They were very high strung, and unfortunately would often run away with Dad and whatever they happened to be pulling at the time—a harrow, a disk, or a wagon. Dad would say, "The damned mules were spooked again by a piece of paper that blew across the field. Took a quarter of a mile to calm them down."

Along with the 60 acres on our farm, Dad rented 30 acres. He planted corn on about 50 acres and wheat on 40 acres. Dad alternated the crops from year to year with an occasional field of alfalfa or red clover, which was plowed under in the fall.

Yields for corn and wheat were modest and always subject to weather conditions. The summer of 1936 was extreme. Temperatures in July and August exceeded 100 degrees almost every day. The barn lot was literally ankle deep in powdery dust. It was fun to run in barefoot, but it got into and onto everything. Mom was a stickler for a clean house, so it was an extra aggravation for her.

Fifty bushels per acre for corn was good and 20 to 30 bushels per acre for wheat was the norm. Today my younger brother gets 170 bushels per acre for corn and 60 for wheat. In the 1930s, corn was worth less than $1 per bushel and wheat a little more, so you can see that an average annual crop would yield perhaps $3,000 to $4,000.

By subtracting the costs of seed, planting, and harvest, Dad may have cleared over $2,000 each year, except in 1936 when everything burned up. I don't recall if my father ever made as much as $5,000. If he did, it was in the late 1950s when yields were better and prices were higher.

Before the 1940s, when automated corn pickers were available, harvesting corn was a long and tedious task. Each ear of corn had to be removed from the stalk *by hand* and tossed into a wagon. The wagon would have a "backboard," which was a raised sideboard on the far side of the wagon against which you could bounce a newly-picked ear of corn. You could hear a steady "clack, clack, clack" of the ears of corn hitting the backboard when everything was going right.

A good man and a disciplined team of horses that would know just when to move the wagon could harvest 100 bushels per day. This was referred to as "shucking" corn. The only tool used was a corn peg, which looked like an old-fashioned beer can opener sewn to a fingerless golf glove. It was used to remove the husk from the ear.

There were corn shucking contests where the best men could remove an ear of corn from its husk and toss it into the wagon in a few seconds. These contests were held even at the state level. The contestants were judged by how many bushels they could shuck in an hour. The winner was a real hero!

It would take a long time to shuck 50 acres of corn, maybe 30 days without help. However, we used hired help. At first, we had a young man who slept in the living room, usually for most of the winter. I don't recall how much Dad paid him in addition to his room and board.

I do remember how much he paid the hired hand he had later, in the 1940s. Paul Wilkerson lived in a rented house down the road about a quarter of a mile away. He had thirteen children. Dad paid him $1 a day as a full-time hired hand. It's incredible to me how his family survived; not only did they do so, but all the kids finished high school and they have all done well. Nobody worked or drank any harder than Mr. Wilkerson. It's interesting that all of his children worked just as hard, but none of them drank.

Threshing was another memorable time on the farm in the 1930s. All the farmers had a binder, which was a horse-drawn machine that cut, bundled, and tied the wheat so that it could be set in bunches, or "shocks." The wheat would ripen in the shocks and we would wait for the steam-powered threshing machine to visit our farm.

Only one farmer in 15 or 20 owned a threshing machine, or separator, as some also called it. Each of the other farmers would take turns having that machine on his farm for a few days. While the thresher was on one farm, the rest of the farmers would bring their flatbed wagons and teams to that place to bring in the wheat to be threshed.

The threshing machine usually was strategically located in a barn lot far away from the previous year's diminishing straw stack. It was also placed far from the house or barn in case of fire.

What a magnificent thing it was to hear and see the steam engine pulling this huge threshing machine down the dirt road to our house! You could see the black smoke from the engine from two miles away. About half an hour after first seeing it, the machine would chug, belch, squeak, and hiss into our barnlot.

Everyone felt important: the man operating the steam engine, my Dad who would direct him to this year's location, my brother Tom and me. You had to be important to have something as massive and awesome as this huge engine and separator to come to your house!

You don't hear the term "cooking for threshers" anymore. In the middle 1930s, my Mom, with the help of the neighbor ladies, *cooked for the threshers*! It was just dinner, the noon meal, but what a meal! There were saw-horses with boards on them that made tables about 20 feet long, accommodating perhaps 30 men plus kids and the helping ladies. We ate fried chicken, mashed potatoes, fresh tomatoes, cucumbers, baked ham, roasted field corn, sweet potatoes, coleslaw, rolls, lots of pies, and gallons of iced tea.

It usually took about three days to finish Dad's crop. Afterwards, the threshing machine would move on and everyone, including Dad and his team of mules and flatbed wagon, would help the next neighbor.

To me, two things were special about threshing time, besides the thrill of the big machinery. One was the ice cream social put on by the farmer whose wheat crop had the highest yield. Dad won it one year and then we were really important.

The second was that Dad would pay the *annual* grocery bill from the proceeds of the wheat crop. Walter Knapp, the local grocer, had carried us and all the other farmers on credit (with no interest) all year until wheat harvest time.

The special thing was that when Dad paid the bill, which was usually about $250, Mr. Knapp let my brother and me have free candy bars. He also gave Mom a half gallon of real ice cream, not the homemade kind. Of course, we ate it immediately, since we had no way to keep it frozen.

This ice cream was from an ice cream company located in Robinson. It is interesting that this company became the Heath Candy Company, now famous for its Heath bars. The company still is located in Robinson, Illinois.

These were great times for us boys, but Dad still couldn't make enough money to stay ahead. He opened a one chair barber shop on the floor above the grocery store in Trimble. He would work all day from sunrise to sunset on the farm, and then cut hair until midnight. He charged 25 cents per haircut, and since it was his shop, he kept it all.

Dad also would cut hair for some people in the basement of our house, but that was an exception. Sam Ellis, who lived in a very remote place from us, would come to the house once a year for a haircut, "whether he needed it or not," Dad would say. Sam never said much, and he looked awful mean to Tom and me. Actually, I guess he was a pretty good guy. He had a family of three or four kids, and they all did well for themselves.

Things started looking up after 1936. Dad bought a tractor, a Massey-Harris four wheel unit. It didn't have a row-crop front wheel, so you could not cultivate corn. However, it could do everything else, such as plow ground, pull the harrow or disc, and pull the wheat drill that planted the wheat.

We also got a car, a 1930 Model A two-door Ford. With the car, a whole new world arrived. We could go to town just about anytime, but all four of us *always* went on Saturday night to the movies.

Mom and Dad would go to the Lincoln Theater, and Tom and I would go the Strand or Grand. These last two theaters always had cowboy movies and serials like the Lone Ranger. Hopalong Cassidy, Jack Steel, and Ken Maynard were our heroes. We each got 15 cents, which covered the movie, which was a dime, and popcorn, which was a nickel.

Mom and Dad went to the Lincoln because it had sophisticated movies about Broadway, love stories and other such drivel. Sometimes there was a Roy Rogers movie, which Tom and I never cared for because Roy never shot anybody.

Tom and I would always go to sleep on the way home. I can remember dozing off and wishing that the trip somehow would take forever. How could it ever get better than going home from a real good time with your Mom and Dad—even Tommy, too!

There were other momentous occasions in the 1930s. One was the 1933 World's Fair in Chicago, which was 200 miles straight north on Route 1. I suppose an eight year-old should remember the fair as an eight year old today would remember Disneyland, but for some reason all I remember is how we got there.

Bud Burris was a sort of jack-of-all-trades, including owning a trucking company that consisted of one stock truck. He would haul hogs to the big market in Chicago. In summer, he would haul watermelons. He also would haul dead rabbits in November.

Most people in our area didn't eat rabbits because quail were easy to get and much better tasting. However, we would hunt rabbits because we could sell them to Bud for ten cents each. In my Dad's case, it paid for his shotgun shells.

Bud would save the rabbits (unrefrigerated) until he had a truck load, then drive to Chicago, park on the street and sell the rabbits for 25 cents each. Some of them were pretty ripe by the time he got to Chicago. A lot of them would be stolen off the truck as he drove slowly through the streets of the city. That was in the early 1930s, and people were just plain hungry.

Bud was an enterprising fellow, and he figured that since a pound is a pound and he charged by the pound to haul hogs, why not people? It would be a convenient and cheap way for many to get to the World's Fair. So, he threw a tarpaulin over the truck bed and we all weighed in. We paid something like five cents a pound and headed for Chicago one night.

There were 30 or 40 people on the truck, including my parents, Tom and me. It took all night to get to Chicago and it rained every inch of the way. I can't recall which time of year it was, but I know I got cold. The water leaked in all over. We were on loose straw with blankets that Mom had brought, but we still got wet and cold.

The only other thing I remember about the trip was the room we had rented in a boarding house—it was clean and warm!

I do recall coming home with a toy Greyhound bus, a rare gift that Dad had found enough money to buy for Tom and me.

Gifts were given very infrequently in our family during the Depression, even at Christmas time. Christmas was just as exciting for my brother and me as it is today for my grandchildren, but it was sometimes disappointing.

One year I remember getting a small paper umbrella, used as favors by my uncle in his job as a salesman for the Ohio Oil Company in Robinson. It was not a very exciting gift for a little boy.

We always went to Trimble Church on Christmas Eve, and it was always packed. Everyone came to see the Christmas pageant put on by the Trimble school children, and to exchange gifts. The "big room" kids performed the Nativity scene. The "little room" children said their "piece:" short poems that each had practiced for weeks before, and then forgot when it came time to stand up before all those people.

At church there was a huge Christmas tree with colored electric lights and gifts all over it. We didn't have a Christmas tree at home. We didn't have electricity so we couldn't have lights, but the real reason was that Dad couldn't afford to buy one.

Parents would bring gifts for their kids and put them on the church tree. The deacons, one with a ladder, and the others handing out gifts, would call off the kids' names. Tom and I would sit on the edge of our seats while Anita Ann King and Betty Lou Conrad's names were called time after time. Other names were called too, but never Tom's or mine.

Everyone eventually got something, though; Tom and I would get a sack of candy, usually peppermint sticks and horehound. The only place I know where you can get real horchound candy now is at the Indianapolis airport at the Little Country Store.

Although some Christmases weren't always great, there were some that were really special.

One time Tom and I wanted BB guns. We were sure it wouldn't happen, but to our delight, we actually got BB guns. This occurred when I was about ten years old. Those guns probably cost $4 or $5 each, which had to have been a real sacrifice for our parents.

But the biggest Christmas ever was a couple of years later. Mom decided to raise turkeys from the local hatchery. She struggled to keep those dumb birds alive and growing. When it rained hard, they would bunch up near the downspout and drown! They would run wildly, especially when the dog chased them, and would kill themselves by running into fences.

By 1938, the road in front of our house had been paved, so somehow the turkeys would get out of their pens and head for the highway. Inevitably, some were run over. Watching Mom chase and retrieve turkeys, and cry sometimes when they would get out of the pens, was for some reason funny to us kids. We never helped much.

Summer finally ended and Mom had thirty or forty turkeys left, which she sold at Thanksgiving for about $2 each.

Christmas came again and, as usual, Tom and I were not counting on much. What we got was a lesson neither of us will ever forget. Mom had worked all summer and fall to raise the turkeys; she used that money to buy each of us a bicycle for Christmas.

My whole family got through the 1930s all right, except for me. In 1938, when I was thirteen years old, I was 5 feet and 10 inches tall, and weighed 120 pounds. I was suffering from my usual hay fever at wheat harvest time, and was sacking wheat on a tractor-pulled combine for my Uncle John.

By that time, the combine had replaced the steam engine and threshing machine. You let the wheat ripen in the field on the stalk and then cut it with the combine, which was also a separator. When you pulled it through the field, it shelled the wheat. The sacker, which was my job, would run the stream of wheat flowing from the machine into two-bushel sacks, tie them and dump them at the corner of the field.

Those sacks full of wheat weighed upwards of 100 pounds each. On a big field with a good yield, I could have four or five sacks to lift and toss over the side of the combine. Uncle John wouldn't slow down, but he also didn't want the sacks scattered, so I strained every muscle in order to unload the grain.

After about ten days of this, one night I had incredible pains in my stomach. Mom assumed that I had pulled a muscle, but it seemed to get worse. Finally, we headed for the local family doctor in Robinson. On the way to town, everything quit hurting. Mom was disgusted with me, but since we were almost at the Allen Baptist Sanitarium, we went on in.

Dr. Allen poked around and decided I probably had been having some gas pains, but he thought he'd take a blood count anyway. It was so high that the doctor had me in surgery in less than an hour to remove a ruptured appendix.

After the operation, the doctor told my parents that the gangrene was so widely spread that I would not live but a few days. He also told them he was going to use a new drug that was a powder which was sprinkled into the wound, but not to count on it doing much.

It turned out that the drug was a new thing called sulfa and it saved my life. I was laid up for several weeks with an open wound that had tubes in it, but I managed to go quail hunting that year anyway.

My dog, Duke, was a very patient pointer. He just let me walk slowly while he held the birds. He had to have been one of the most talented bird dogs ever. I once saw him point to a live bird while holding a freshly killed one in his mouth. Today I'd give a great deal of money for him.

Attending high school was quite an accomplishment for the kids in southern Illinois in the 1930s. I can recall that in the seventh and eighth grades, we students would talk about who would go to high school. For me, there was never any doubt. Even if I had entertained thoughts of not attending high school, it was a given with my parents. College was something else, and was in fact out of the question.

The issue of attending or not attending was based on economics. Perhaps half of the students in Trimble grade school couldn't go to high school because of the cost. Clothes, books and transportation were too expensive. There were no school buses. You had to walk or own a car, which most people didn't have. It was five miles to Robinson, which was too far to walk in winter or ride a bicycle.

Yet, although high school was an economic consideration, none of us mentioned that as an explanation. Those who announced that they weren't going gave reasons such as: they'd soon be getting married (after all, the girls were going on 16 years), they were needed on the farm (very true in some cases) or they planned to take a job where a high school diploma didn't matter.

The truth was that they all wanted very much to go to high school. I'll never forget Wanda Brock, the smartest girl in the class, announcing that she wasn't going to high school. We all understood, because Mr. Brock was awfully poor compared to some of us.

High school was certainly a new and somewhat frightening experience for me, at first. None of my eighth grade friends made it to high school.

That also was when my name started to become a slightly annoying problem, especially when the speech teacher was teaching us to remember names by association. She picked Jimmy Woodworth as an example, and of course related his name to the word, "wood." The class snickered for ten minutes before the teacher caught on. She was as embarrassed as I was.

As a freshman, I wasn't big enough to play football or basketball. Instead, I got into the school plays and had a lot of fun being an amateur actor.

I was never accepted by the town students, who dominated most everything, including school plays. These were a group of boys and girls who had gone through grade school together. They formed a social clique, and there was no place for a gawky farm kid with that bunch.

I had just about then caught on to what sex was all about, but I had the distinct impression that those folks not only knew about sex but practiced it a lot. If this is not true, I'll apologize right now to all those not guilty.

Going through high school was not all that eventful or difficult for me. I never took a book home, in part because we didn't have electric lights. While I could have seen well enough by the kerosene lamp, I just didn't do it. I still made almost straight A's in high school.

Math was the only semi-technical course I took because I thought I could someday become a bookkeeper. Most of my studies in high school were liberal arts-oriented, including Speech, English, Latin, Geography, and American and World History.

In my junior and senior years, I took typing because the prettiest girl in the school was in that class. She had come to school in her junior year as a transfer student from Oklahoma. The first time I saw her, I was in study hall with my best friend, John Johnson. I took one look at her and told Johnny that someday I would marry this girl.

I spent most of my junior year simply trying to get a date with this pretty brunette, whose name was Jeanette Crossman. Believe it or not, she worked in a Woolworth's 5 & 10-cent store, just like in the song.

That summer, I would go in the store on Saturday night, buy candy and ask for a date. The usual answer was "no," but there was a different reason every time. Obviously, the girl didn't care for me.

Early in my senior year, I finally succeeded in getting a date to take her to the movies. We went to the Lincoln Theater to see Gene Kelly and Alice Faye, and then we went to the Sugar Bowl for a malt after the movie.

After taking my date home, I was on my way home in my Dad's 1936 V-8 (we had upgraded from the Model A.) I was in such a dream world that I didn't notice a car coming straight at me on the main highway. He hit me almost head on at about 60 m.p.h., and I had been doing about 30. Both cars were totaled, but both drivers came out with only a few bad bruises. A heck of a way to end my first date, but it showed how much in love I was.

In 1940, my younger brother Joe was born. Joe turned out to be the only one among us brothers who cared for farming. Tom and I left home for military service when Joe was only three years old. Neither Tom nor I ever lived at home on the farm after that.

Tom and I have admired our "kid" brother for his accomplishments. Soon after he finished high school, Joe got married and worked at odd jobs away from home.

Joe found a job at the local Marathon Oil refinery in Robinson. He worked eight-hour shifts, sometimes at night. Joe also found enough time during daylight hours to do farm labor, using some of Dad's equipment.

Joe made enough money to build a nice house next door to our folks' home, and started farming Dad's land. He also rented and farmed other people's land. Eventually, Joe bought land of his own. Between his own land and land that he rents, Joe now farms nearly 1,000 acres.

During my high school days, an important event occurred: World War II started! Everybody in the country knew it started on Sunday, December 7, 1941. However, I didn't find out until I went to school on Monday, since there was no electricity, and therefore no radio at my house!

Within a week, our school principal, Ralph Stringer, was standing in front of the school assembly in his captain's uniform, saying goodbye to all 400 students of Robinson High. He was old (34 years) but was quite a figure in his uniform.

All the girls cried. The boys cheered and couldn't wait to join him in the service of their country. Some seniors were already planning to enlist and did so before finishing their last year in school.

During the summer of 1943, after our spring crops were planted, I got a job working on the state road gang for 60 cents per hour, ten hours each day. Jeanette and I had broken up for some reason, and besides, she was going off to college. I really hadn't changed my mind about marrying her some day, but at this particular time things just weren't working out.

Six dollars a day, six days a week, is thirty-six dollars. That was more money than I had ever seen, and more than enough to do anything and everything in Robinson and the surrounding area.

Betty Lou Conrad and I dated that whole summer and took in every county fair around. We rode every carnival ride there was. I saw Betty Lou at Mom's funeral 45 years later and introduced her to my two handsome sons. She told them I was a great date because I was the only boy she knew who could go on the wildest rides without throwing up. I considered that a real compliment.

While Betty Lou was a pretty girl and a lot of fun, I still thought Jeanette Crossman was special. So, when Jeanette's folks invited me to go with them to visit her in college at Shurtliff in Alton, Illinois, I jumped at the chance.

It was awful! She had a group of new friends who were really sophisticated. The boys were all 4F, the girls all smoked and I sure hoped they weren't like the high school city kids I had known earlier. Jeanette ignored me during the entire day.

I came home and decided to enlist before my draft call, since my draft number had come up that summer. I had my draft number but hadn't been inducted.

II

THE ENGINEER

I decided to join the Navy V-6, a program where the Navy would send me through college in preparation for becoming a Navy officer. This was similar to today's ROTC, and it looked like a good deal to me. However, I flunked the physical exam, because the Navy said I had an overbite. I don't know why that disqualified me, but I guess it would have been unbecoming of a Navy officer to have an overbite.

I then tried to join the Army Air Corps. I wanted to be a pilot. The Army paid no attention to the overbite, and scheduled me to officially join the Army and become a candidate for the aviation cadet program. That was in October, 1943, but I didn't have to report for duty until December.

That same October, Jeanette had an emergency appendix operation. Her folks asked me again if I would go with them to Alton, where she was in the hospital. This time she was happy to see me. She left college and came home to Robinson to recover. After that, we dated again—usually movies at the Lincoln—until I left for the Air Corps in December.

My Army career was about as unheroic as could be. I went through basic training at Biloxi, Mississippi in December, 1943. I have never been as cold before or since then.

Those first few months of being away from home for the first time were pretty traumatic.

Homesickness is not a fun experience, but I wasn't alone. Most of the guys in my barracks were from Brooklyn, including a fellow named Neil Simon, who later wrote a popular play about that time, called "Biloxi Blues." It's funny that I don't recall seeing as much prejudice as came through in the play. I'm sure it was there, but to a country boy, a Brooklyn Jew was no different than any other big-city kid. I liked the city folk and became good friends with several.

I qualified for the aviation cadet program and pilot training. Before I was to start pre-flight training, however, the Army felt that an officer-to-be must have some college education. I was sent to the University of Florida for one quarter, where I studied physics, chemistry, and college algebra.

After CTD (College Training Detachment), I went to "on the line training" to await classroom space at pre-flight school in Montgomery, Alabama. This decision was rooted in the problem that the Army had too many pilots in early 1944. They had too many pilots and not enough infantry to invade Normandy.

Part of the solution to that problem was to take some aviation cadets out of their flight training program, give them six weeks of field training, and send them to England as privates, each with his own rifle. The Army had an easy way to decide who stayed in the flight program and who went to the infantry. Those who had volunteered for the service stayed in cadet training, and those who had been inducted into the service got a rifle.

My records showed that I had been inducted, so I was to go with the infantry. When this was announced, I was given one day to pack up and ship out. I realized that I had to talk to someone fast, for although my draft number had indeed been called in October, 1943, I had volunteered for the Air Corps before I was to report for Army service.

With less than an hour before departure, I got an audience with the major in charge and convinced him I was not an inductee, I was a *volunteer* inductee. I stayed in the cadet program with the others that were left.

I have often thought how that event changed my life and my whole career. Many of my buddies got shot in June, 1944. While that may not have happened to me, I would not have otherwise been exposed to aviation, and probably would not have started my career in that industry.

Later in 1944, the Army still had too many pilots. My classification was changed to "candidate for bombardier." To become a bombardier, I had to go through gunnery school, so I was shipped to Tyndall Field in Panama City, Florida, to learn how to shoot.

The first part of gunnery training was skeet shooting with Model 12 Winchester shot guns. I had never seen skeet targets, but they looked awfully easy to hit compared to a quail flying at full speed through the brush. I don't think I missed a single skeet bird.

Later, of course, we fired 50 caliber machine guns at tow targets. Each of us were given differently colored bullets that had been dipped in paint. Every time the tow target was checked, it was full of my color.

We also fired "photo" guns at fighters, which involved aiming gunsights at movies of our targets. Our class was one of the first to fire a "disintegrating" bullet at Bell King Cobra fighters that were equipped with a sensing device to record hits. These so-called "disintegrating" bullets would sometimes lodge in the control surfaces of the fighters and cause some real problems.

Near the end of gunnery school, I was called to the office of the commanding officer of Tyndall Field. I can't recall whether he was a colonel or a general, but he was awesome to me. I couldn't imagine what I had done wrong or if something was wrong at home.

He asked me where I learned to shoot, and other questions about where I was from, and so on. Finally, he said I had as close to a perfect score as anyone ever had in the gunnery school. I was named "Gunner of the Class!" This got me a nice certificate and a pass to go on leave back home for a week.

I was 19 years old and on my way home in uniform. It seemed to me that the thing to do was to become engaged. So, I made a down payment on a $120 diamond ring and proposed to Jeanette as soon as I got home. She accepted, but we decided to wait until the war was over to set a wedding date. That was a short week but certainly a happy one.

I returned to Tyndall Field to learn that we were heading for more "on the line training" to await the start of bombardier training. Some time later, the Army decided it had too many bombardiers, so I was sent off to Selman Field to learn how to become a navigator.

We trained all through the summer of 1945. About the time we were to graduate, I got hurt in a touch football game and ended up in the hospital for a couple of weeks. While I was in the hospital, the atomic bomb was dropped on Japan. The war was over.

I got out of the hospital and found that my classmates had received their commissions. They were scheduled for occupation duty in Europe. The navigation school was closing at Selman, so to finish my two weeks of training, I had to go to Arlington Field outside Houston, Texas.

I finished training, had purchased my officer uniform and assumed I would be sent to Europe with my previous classmates. But then, the Army gave me a choice. Take my commission and stay in the service for two to three years, or go home right then as a private!

I had trained for two years to be an Air Corps officer, so it was hard to turn down those gold bars. However, the government had announced the G.I. Bill, which meant free college. That was an opportunity I wouldn't pass up. I could go home, marry Jeanette, and get paid to go to college!

I wanted to be an engineer and get into the aircraft industry. The Rose Polytechnic Institute in Terre Haute was only 40 miles from home, and it was one of the best engineering schools in the country. Jeanette could get a job in Terre Haute, so we would have extra money. Probably, we could even save some!

At Arlington Field, I was given travel pay to go from Houston to Terre Haute. I think I got something over $100, maybe $150.

One of my buddies was traveling in the same direction as me; he was bound for Ohio and I for southern Illinois. We got into a poker game the night before we were to take the train home.

I was a pretty good draw and stud poker player. My Dad had made extra money playing poker at the local Moose Club during the 1930s. He was not only good, he was close to being a professional. He had taught Tommy and me how to play poker and bridge.

However, Dad had never introduced me to a game called "Red Dog." Both my buddy and I lost practically every cent we had in that game the night before we were to head home.

It was no big deal! We simply decided to hitchhike the 1,000 miles home. We ended up hitchhiking day and night, riding in every conceivable kind of vehicle and being picked up by all sorts of people.

We had been dropped off in the middle of Oklahoma by a rancher at 2:00 a.m. the first morning. After about two hours, we were ready to ride with anybody. When a guy in a 1933 Ford V-8 picked us up, we were grateful.

It turned out that he was very drunk. The first thing that happened was that we hit a cow. We didn't even slow down, and had relatively minor damage.

The second thing that happened was that our driver missed a left turn entering the town of Okmulgee and ended up on the front porch of a house. My buddy and I got out of the car unhurt. We walked away down the main street before anyone came out to see what was going on.

We finally arrived in East St. Louis, where we were so exhausted that we stayed in a boarding house that cost about $3 or $4 per night. After a good rest in East St. Louis, we started out again on Route 40.

We got a ride with a very nice older couple driving a 1940 Buick. They were on their way to *Ohio*, right through Terre Haute, which was only 40 miles from home. I got out in Marshall, Illinois, and walked most of the 20 miles down Route 1 to our house.

What a great feeling to be home after two years! While I had experienced relatively little of the war, it had been quite a time for an 18 year-old farm kid who had never been farther away from home than Terre Haute, not counting the World's Fair in 1933.

The first thing I did after I got home was to apply for admission to Rose Poly. It turned out that I would not have been eligible were it not for the credits I had earned at the University of Florida while I was in the Army.

I entered a program that would give me a degree in mechanical engineering in 36 months, straight through, no breaks or vacation. As it turned out, the G.I. Bill paid tuition, books, and $90 per month cash, and I had been awarded this for exactly 36 months. How lucky can you get?

Jeanette and I decided to get married in March, 1946. At that time, I was a college freshman. Jeanette had a job making about $20 per week in Terre Haute with the Commercial Credit Corporation. As a married G.I., I would get a raise to $105 per month.

In Terre Haute, we had a two-room apartment, with one bedroom and a kitchen. We shared a bathroom and refrigerator with two other couples. We had enough money to buy a car, which we did: a 1929 Ford Model A. On weekends, we would drive from Terre Haute to one of our folk's places.

We even upgraded to a newer car, a 1936 Ford V-8 coupe. What a car! It ran like a clock and was just the thing for a prospering newlywed couple.

This prosperity lasted until the end of my sophomore year, when our son John was born. Now Jeanette couldn't work, so we had a choice: stop college, get a job somewhere, and live reasonably comfortably, or try to get by on our $105 per month for two years.

We had no savings and were making payments on the car. We decided to sell the car and try to stick it out until I graduated. We paid $45 per month rent on a bigger apartment in Terre Haute about two miles from the school. I hitchhiked to school.

We lived on the G.I. Bill stipend, which left only $60 per month for food, medicine and other essentials. We didn't eat a lot. As a matter of fact, I weighed 129 pounds when I graduated. That's not much for someone six feet tall.

College was not easy for me, nothing like the easy time I had in high school. I was on probation the last quarter of my sophomore year, with something near a 2.0 (out of 4.0) average.

My junior and senior years went much better. My senior year was especially good, with close to a 3.5 average. This brought my grade average for the last three years up to around 2.5.

Still, this average was not very good compared to those of many whiz kids in my class of sixty students. My class consisted of students majoring in the disciplines of chemical, civil, electrical and mechanical engineering.

Graduation was in January, 1949. I honestly don't know how I ever made it through those 36 months. I would have quit more than once, but Jeanette wouldn't let me. She certainly understood far better than I what a college degree was going to mean to us. She earned my Bachelor of Science in Mechanical Engineering as much as I did.

In 1948 and 1949, jobs weren't all that plentiful. I had one interview with the Ball Shoe Company in Michigan City, Indiana, for a position as a time study engineer. This job would involve counting the operations that some union employee was performing to see if you can figure a way to make him work harder.

The only other interview I had was for the position of draftsman at the Naval Ordnance Plant in Indianapolis. As it turned out, the only offer I was given was for the job at the Naval Ordnance facility. It paid $2,900 per year, which was a weekly take-home pay of $48, or almost double what I'd made the previous three years.

I took the job, but didn't have enough money to move all of us to Indianapolis. I borrowed $20 from Mom, who was by then working as a pastry cook in a small restaurant in Robinson. Jeanette and John moved in with her folks. I went to Indianapolis and rented a room, planning to send for my wife and son as soon as I got a couple of paychecks.

I had enough money after a month to rent a three-room apartment. Then, Jeanette and John came to Indianapolis and I started my career in aircraft instrument development.

The apartment was in a poor part of town. It had a coal-fired furnace which was in a basement dug out of the clay. There was no cement floor. Water from the ground would leak into the basement, and then into the ash box of the furnace. Fortunately, water did not get into the burner, so we could keep a fire going.

The place also had big rats! I used Johnny's toy baseball bat to kill rats in the kitchen, where they seemed to like being around the gas stove.

To go from that place ultimately to a million-dollar home in New Canaan, Connecticut comes close to defining what success is. However, many other things occurred during the intervening 30 years that make me feel that my life was truly successful.

The Navy Department instrument manufacturing plant in Indianapolis was called NOPI (Naval Ordnance Plant—Indianapolis.) It was probably one of the finest light manufacturing factories in the world at that time. It had been built during the war to manufacture the Norden bomb sight. In 1949, it produced electronics for ships and aircraft.

The Norden Company still played a major part of the product development for NOPI. I could not have picked a better place to learn aircraft electronics.

My first task was to copy, on vellum, in ink, several faded blueprints of circuits for a shipboard fire control system. It took me a year! It was a lousy job, but I was afraid to complain. I would never have done so anyway, because I'd been taught that you never do that.

I decided that the best way out of this assignment was to do it as best as I could, and keep my eyes open for something better.

In 1950, the Norden Company had developed a new high altitude (50,000 ft.) bombing system which had a "computer" as the brain of the system.

This computer was not only analog, it was a *mechanical* analog computer. All of the mathematical functions required to calculate the bomb trajectory was done through the positioning of rotating dials and metal shafts. These functions also included corrections and calculations for wind, air density, air speed, temperature, angle of attack, and the altitudes of aircraft and target.

At the time, most of us working on the system knew nothing of modern digital bits or bytes. Since it was completely mechanical, tolerances for part size and fit had to be extremely tight, in order to achieve some semblance of accuracy. I don't recall the bombing accuracy of this device, but it must have been within several hundred yards. Therefore, it would have been ineffective for dropping any weapon other than an atomic bomb.

The thing was, in fact, a mechanical monster. The computer unit alone was made up of approximately twenty major components which were interconnected by rotating shafts and couplings. The integrators were ball-and-disc mechanical units, and even the *amplifiers* were mechanical! Altogether, this machine weighed 200 pounds and measured about 2 feet by 5 feet by 3 feet. Moreover, it didn't work most of the time.

I volunteered to become an operator in the test lab for the system. At that time, no one wanted such a lowly job. Besides, none of the versions of the system had passed the tests, so one didn't get a feeling of accomplishment.

I got the testing job almost as soon as I asked for it. The first thing I did was to meet with some of the visiting Norden engineers and learn everything there was to know about the system. The Norden engineers said nobody else in NOPI ever had done this. After all, NOPI was just a manufacturing facility; why should anyone there need to understand the design?

Once I understood the device, it was easy to figure out why none of the units passed the final tests. Part of the problem was that the couplings didn't line up between the components. At that time, the components were rebuilt until the couplings were perfectly aligned. This process, considering the buildup of tolerances, depended on pure luck.

To obtain perfect alignment more reliably, I had the couplings made separately from the shafts. After the parts were assembled, they were adjusted to line up by loosening or tightening a set screw. Once they were lined up, I had them drilled and pinned by one of the superb German technicians who worked in the lab.

We soon had many computer units going through production and successfully passing tests. They were then shipped to Patuxent River, Maryland for installation in Navy aircraft.

I got promoted in grade every few months, until in less than three years I was a GS-11 making about $5000 per year.

After four years, I became head of the bombing system project, with responsibility for design modification, manufacturing, and testing, as well as being the installation consultant to Patuxent River. I was also liaison to Norden in White Plains, New York. This job started my first travels to places like Washington, D.C. and New York City.

I got to meet some pretty important people, like the co-managers of Norden Laboratories. This is the only company I've known which had two equally ranking people running the company. One was a technical person and the other had a finance background. They got along together great and ran the company very well, as I recall.

I'll never forget my first meeting with the high-ranking officer from Washington who had responsibility for NOPI. It was shortly after I had found the solution to the computer problem, so I was still living on $45 per week, and was not exactly the best dressed fellow around.

I remember having two dress shirts and one suit, which I always wore to work with one of the shirts and a tie. Jeanette would wash and iron one shirt every day. The collars would fray, so she would take them off, turn them around and sew them back on.

The day I was to meet this admiral, I wanted to look presentable. Just before I was to go to the head office, I went to the men's room to comb my hair and adjust my tie. I flipped the collar up to tighten the tie and the collar came off! I looked like the local butcher.

Being an enterprising fellow, I went to my desk and got a stapler. In the men's room, I stapled my collar back on in time to meet the admiral. I didn't move my head around much, because the staples scratched a bit.

My boss at NOPI was Paul Blodgett, an amazingly energetic fellow, considering he had a heart problem so serious that he had purple fingernails. Besides being a sharp guy who was very helpful to a green engineer, Paul was an avid and excellent golfer.

I joined the plant golf league, and with a set of wood-shafted clubs which had belonged to my father-in-law, I learned how to play the greatest game in the world.

Golf was relatively expensive even in the early 1950s, and I played with minimum equipment: no golf shoes, no glove, and sometimes I'd play a round with *one* ball. I never thought about losing it. I guess I would have had to quit the round if I had lost the ball.

In 1952, Jeanette was pregnant with our second son, Steven. It was a very difficult pregnancy and there were a number of visits to the house by the doctor. He decided that part of the problem was that she was closed in at the house most of the time.

I was involved with people at work, and the doctor knew I played golf once a week and occasionally went fishing or hunting. He demanded that I take Jeanette out to dinner once a week, which would have cost at least $5. There was no way we could do that, even though I knew he was probably at least partly correct.

We did manage to get out some, but certainly didn't spend that kind of money. While we had more than we did during school, we still were not living high on the hog.

I remember one Christmas when I splurged and bought Jeanette a *vacuum cleaner*! I paid sixty dollars for it at Sears; $5 down and payments of $5 per month.

Steven was born in September, 1952. Now we were contributing to the baby boom.

III

"DOWN TO LEARS"

By the beginning of 1953, my job at NOPI seemed to have stopped at the GS-11 level. I was getting a little bored. I also was concerned that I would get in the rut of government service. I didn't want to become part of an evolving bureaucracy that wouldn't recognize individual performance or offer any real incentive to perform at all.

In March, I started looking for a new job. This led to an interview with a visiting recruiter from the Lear Company in Grand Rapids, Michigan.

I was offered a job as a product engineer at $136 per week, which was $7,000 per year. This was pretty good pay for 1953. I took the job, and we moved to Grand Rapids. There we rented a neat two-bedroom bungalow in a nice neighborhood on Hazen Street.

Before the family had moved, I had reported to work at Lear, Inc. I was housed by the company at the "Lear House," which I learned was one of Bill Lear's many personal residences around the country.

About the second evening there, I was in the kitchen when I heard several people arrive. Pretty soon this fellow in his middle 40s burst into the kitchen, asked me my name, and wanted to know if I'd like a hamburger. It was Bill Lear and his ever-present entourage of co-pilot and cronies. Bill fixed hamburgers and we all had a great time.

I had met the famous William P. Lear, Sr. on my second day with the company, and he had fixed my dinner!

I think that Lear, Inc. was generating revenue of about $20 million per year in 1953. It was a public company, but was not on the Big Board at that time.

Bill Lear had just won the Collier Trophy, presented to him by President Harry Truman, for inventing the first practical autopilot for jet aircraft. He had accomplished this in typical Bill Lear fashion, which follows.

The Lear company had built wing flap actuators, which moved the wing flaps up and down, and other electromechanical components during and after the war. Bill Lear had moved the company from Ohio to Grand Rapids, which had been a center for furniture manufacturing and consequently a very low cost labor area.

Most of the company's business was conducted with the Air Force through the Wright-Patterson facility and field in Dayton, Ohio.

Bill was on one of his many visits to Wright-Patterson in the early 1950s, when he heard the "brass" complaining that the Westinghouse Corporation had failed to meet specifications for an autopilot for jet fighters. Bill Lear had responded by promising to deliver a fully operating autopilot in a matter of weeks. The Air Force took him up on the offer.

On the way back to Grand Rapids, Lear was reported to have said, "How in the hell do you design a gyroscope?"

Bill worked his team of engineers day and night. With some innovative ideas, like magnetic powder clutches for control surfaces and electrolytic gravity sensors for the gyroscopes, he put together an autopilot system which worked.

As a result, Bill won the production contract from the Air Force, along with the Collier Trophy.

My first task at Lear, Inc. was more or less self-assigned. When the autopilot gyroscope was used to determine the vertical navigation reference, the electrolytic gravity sensors had a "dead spot" near center, which means that there was poor signal strength. The vertical position seemed to wander, so everyone assumed that the problem was with the sensors.

As was the case at NOPI, I found that most of the people concerned with supporting a product in production knew very little about the theory behind the product. I found the gyroscope's designers, and tried to talk with them about the problem. They were now working on new devices, and wouldn't dream of helping the manufacturing staff.

These engineers' attitude was that the design was perfect. Therefore, the problem had to be in manufacturing; let manufacturing solve it! Management wouldn't assign the design engineers the task of helping, even temporarily. This was because the designers would be offended by such a menial task. They might quit! In some cases, this would have been the best thing for the company.

The design people finally agreed to spend time educating me in gyroscopic theory. I think they did it to get rid of me.

Gyroscopes are interesting devices. They were first used as navigational aids on ships. A "gyro" is a spinning mass, like a wheel spinning around its hub, or center.

Depending upon the speed of rotation and its mass (weight), a gyroscope maintains its position very rigidly. When properly spinning, it would always point its spin axis, or hub, at the same point in distant space.

On a ship, if one had such a spinning mass encased in gimbals which allowed freedom of movement, one could point the axis north with a magnet. The deviation of the ship's direction of movement from magnetic north would then allow the navigator to determine the ship's heading.

This is exactly what was done with ship's gyroscopes at that time. They were very large, measuring several feet in diameter and weighing hundreds of pounds.

The same principle can be applied to aircraft navigation, using a much smaller mass. The gyroscope typically would be a few inches in diameter, but it would spin much faster, in order to obtain a high, stable "inertia." The combination of speed of rotation and mass results in a rigid position, just as in the ship.

In aircraft, however, one has to know not only the direction (heading), but also whether one is flying up or down (pitch), or rolling (roll). The deviation from level flight can be measured from a gyroscope which has its axis pointing straight up (vertical).

When a gyroscope is mounted in two gimbals that are at right angles to each other, one can measure pitch and roll using the same method used to indicate heading. Thus, aircraft have two types of gyroscopes, the directional gyro and the vertical gyro.

Gyros tend to "drift" off their position, due to forces created by friction in the gimbal bearings or from poor gimbal balance. To keep a directional gyro pointing to north, one uses the signal from a magnetic sensor (compass). This applies what is called a "precession" force to the gyro, always bringing it back to north when it drifts away.

The same principle is applied to a vertical gyro, except one uses a gravity sensor. This could be a pendulum or a mercury bubble that measures the deviation from vertical. It generates the precession force to keep the gyro axis pointing vertically.

As a result of this education, I got the idea to set up a weights-and-balance system. I had the gravity sensor wired to torque motors to counter any "off-balance" condition. Without describing the whole jury-rigged system, just let me say that it worked. It proved how very sensitive the gravity sensor was, and that the null or "dead" spot had to come from something else in the gyroscope.

With my newfound knowledge of the sensor and my "education" in gyroscopes, further investigation showed that the problem was the friction level of the gimbal bearings. The friction level was directly affected by the pre-load of the bearings. Pre-load is the force between the inner and outer races of a ball bearing.

I also determined that pre-loads were correct. Therefore, the unacceptable null or dead spot was *inherent in the design*! In other words, a perfectly manufactured unit was within the specifications of the contract, but barely.

The cost and poor yield (the number of units passing testing) of the product was "killing" the company. Our only answer was either to re-design the product, or negotiate with the Air Force for a more liberal specifications.

I first looked at the military specifications. That's when I discovered a very interesting thing. The military specs allowed twice as much "dead spot" as our manufacturing specs!

The military (customer) specification allowed the gyro accuracy around vertical to be in error up to one-half of a degree.

A manufacturing specification is usually more stringent than the customer specification. This avoids the rejection of units that are marginally close to the maximum allowable error due to slight differences in testing equipment or human interpretation of equipment readings.

Typically, contractors use a ten percent margin from the maximum allowable error. However, in this case the Lear designers had arbitrarily specified a 50 percent margin. This imposed a real burden on the manufacturing department.

In fact, the one-quarter degree accuracy imposed on manufacturing was beyond the limit of the design capability of the gyro. This meant that only a small percentage of the units would pass testing. The units which would pass testing would be those that had a buildup of tolerances which compensated each other in a way better than the theoretical design capability.

Now, allowing for a margin in design to conform to requirements is one thing, but "achieving quality" by tightening specifications beyond the inherent design capability is stupid and almost fraudulent to the company.

We went to the Air Force, showed them that we could open our internal test specifications, improve our yields, and stay well within their requirements. In other words, our product would "fly the airplane" safely and adequately.

I gained much respect and a great deal of trust from our Air Force customers, because we never had needed to show them any of this. After all, we did meet their specifications. I felt it was something they deserved to know. Moreover, the gyroscopes they would now receive were on the average not as accurate in showing vertical as those we previously had been shipping.

This was not my first lesson in honesty and openness, but it was a very rewarding one. The customer trusted me and my company, the real requirement was determined, the company could make more money, the product cost went down enough to pass on some of it to the customer, and a new young production engineering manager at Lear had one of his biggest problems solved. His name was Thomas G. Kamp, a name I'll come back to later.

This incident taught me something else early in my career. A great number of problems encountered in running a company are self-imposed. The arbitrary manufacturing specification for the gyros is a good example.

I also learned that "quality" is defined by satisfying a customer with product, service, and attention, and that meeting requirements, not exceeding them, is the key to economic success.

All this had taken place during my first year at Lear. We still lived in the little house on Hazen Street in Grand Rapids. We had upgraded our car from the 1948 Plymouth we bought in Indianapolis to a 1951 Dodge with a fluid drive transmission—the predecessor to the automatic transmission.

Jeanette and I thought nothing of loading Johnny and Steven in the car on a Friday after work and driving ten hours to Robinson to spend the weekend with one of our folks, especially if it were quail season.

Dad was still struggling on the farm and not making more than three or four thousand dollars a year. All Mom could talk about was the rumors that the power company might bring power down the road past our place, so she could get "lights." Running water was still not something to count on.

In 1955, Mom got her electricity. There were only six houses on the three mile road between Trimble and Gordon, and three of these homes decided not to "sign up." I don't know why the power company actually put up the lines. I swear Mom wished so hard for it to happen that it just happened.

Dad didn't seem to care much for electricity, and wasn't about to pay for appliances such as toasters, a refrigerator or radio. He probably just didn't have the money. So, Mom got a job as a pastry cook at Bud Burris's diner in Robinson, at a minimum wage of less than $3 per hour. Yes, this was the same Bud Burris who took us to the World's Fair in 1933.

From her wages, Mom managed to buy the appliances she'd always wanted, and even managed to buy herself a car. It was the beginning of better times for my parents.

Jeanette's parents always had prospered with her Dad's job as a foreman at the local Marathon refinery. They had a new house near the Robinson High School and lived a very comfortable life. I thought if I could ever approach Jeanette's father's status in life, I'd really have it made.

A third great event was happening in our lives. Jeanette was pregnant again, this time with Susan. Babies seemed to be coming *routinely.*

Sue was born on January 25, 1954 at Blodgett Hospital. She was the prettiest newborn baby in the world. I'm sure my kids will be disappointed that I don't write a lot about them in this book, but none of the other three will take issue with my saying that Susan has been the perfect daughter through every stage, including her days now as a mother of three. She has the very best traits of her mother and her grandmother Titsworth, my Mom.

The next couple of years at Lear were rather uneventful. In Grand Rapids, if you worked at Lear, Inc., you worked "down to Lears." This was just a local expression, best pronounced in a good Midwestern twang. It was a great place to be employed as an engineer.

My job title was "product support engineer." This meant that I had engineering responsibility for products in manufacturing. Specifically, I oversaw the production of gyroscopes, which probably represented 20 percent of the annual revenue of the company.

The company lived for several years off the revenues generated by the autopilot and vertical gyro indicator products. Both products had been designed in the early 1950s.

Bill Lear lived in Pacific Palisades, California, and would show up three or four times each year in Grand Rapids. He didn't care much for the military products operations in Grand Rapids. His love was commercial aircraft and related aircraft instruments.

Bill loved publicity, as evidenced by his flying to Moscow in a twin-engine Cessna, loaded with modern Lear equipment, in the mid-1950s. He simply filed a flight plan out of Berlin and flew to Moscow. It sure shook up the military.

Bill also modified a number of Lockheed Lodestars. He renamed them LearStars and set a lot of commercial aircraft cross-country speed records. We had a LearStar in Grand Rapids; it was a great airplane, being fast, quiet, comfortable, and reliable.

Like many companies, Lear, Inc. in Grand Rapids had its cliques and factions. Engineering essentially consisted of two groups: "Advanced Engineering" and the rest of us. Advanced Engineering worked on such things as three-gyro platforms and inertial platforms for missiles. We in "Retarded Engineering" continued to work on the stuff that paid the bills.

Engineers are never satisfied with the design of a product. That is an exemplary attribute, for otherwise we would never have anything new.

The problem is that engineers are not often the best businessmen.

The engineer's goal is to make a better mousetrap, and it may not even resemble the old one. When a new and better product is developed, there is a natural temptation to put it into production quickly. Pressures to do so are put on managers by the designers, who want to see their latest project succeed.

Marketing also pressures management, often saying that the "marketing window" of opportunity is narrow. What they mean is that time is short before the competition brings out a similar or better product.

Too often, management ignores the new startup costs of manufacturing, the benefits to the customer of the lower costs of the original product that came with the higher production volume, or the better customer service which came with experience.

It is sometimes more advantageous to the manufacturer *and* the customer to make design modifications to the original product. This can be better than replacing the original product with a completely new product, even if it is "superior" to the first.

The balance of timing the next generations of product against the new replacement of products is what managing high-tech product companies is all about. However, even in the 1950s, companies were eager to "end of life" the first generation of product. Understand, I have nothing against basic research or new ideas, but to abandon your meal ticket for promises is a good way to go hungry.

Our "retarded" engineers had been working on a two-gyro platform, using conventional two-axis gyros of the type we were manufacturing as individual vertical and directional units. The two units were mounted in a common roll gimbal, which was servo-driven by the roll sensor on the vertical gyro. This product could provide all the information for an autopilot and the heading indicator, as well as the artificial two-axis attitude indicator (pitch and roll).

The Gyro Engineering department was working on this two-gyro device while the Indicator Design group was working an a three-axis indicator; one instrument to show pitch, roll, and heading on the same ball. My brother, Tom, was in the Indicator Design group.

Tom had also gone to Rose Poly for a time, then to the University of Illinois, and then to a design school in St. Louis. He never got his bachelor's degree but instead became a product designer—a trade we don't have any more and one we badly need. Tom had followed me to NOPI as a draftsman and then later came to Lear as a "designer." He was a better engineer than most, and the fact that he had no degree didn't hurt him at Lear. After all, Bill Lear had only an eighth grade education!

Tom contributed greatly to the design of the first three-axis indicator. Later, in 1970, he was honored by NASA for the design of the Apollo all-attitude three-axis indicator used on the Apollo moon missions.

While all this was going on, the Air Force and Navy were looking for an answer to a major problem associated with very low-level bombing using atomic weapons. The problem of a low-level drop of an atomic bomb was simply that while you could hit the target, the plane and crew went up in the same explosion that devastated the target.

The military came up with the clever idea of a so-called "wings-level" approach, where the aircraft would approach the target, pull up in a steep climb while keeping the wings level, and release the bomb at some high angle (60 to 80 degrees).

The plane would literally "toss" the bomb, then do an Immelmann maneuver that would reverse the aircraft's direction and get the hell out of the area before the bomb finished its upward and then downward path to the target.

Clever, huh? Yes, but an ordinary vertical gyroscope is limited in its ability to show pitch and roll accurately above a pitch angle of 60 degrees.

When a high performance aircraft, like a fighter, reaches a pitch angle above 60 degrees, a conventional vertical gyroscope starts to rotate about its roll axis at high speed. The gyro loses its stability when its spinning rotor lines up parallel to the roll axis. This is called "gimbal lock."

From that point on, if one has gimbal lock, the gyro is useless. Such a condition can be brought on even when the aircraft does something simple, like a loop. To avoid this problem, the gyro is forced to rotate more slowly before the pitch reaches 60 degrees.

As the aircraft continues to pitch up, as when making an Immelmann or loop, the gyro rotates slowly around roll. It would not show proper pitch or roll information during those maneuvers, but the gyro would maintain its rigidity and accuracy when the aircraft returned to a pitch attitude of less than 60 degrees.

In effect, the gyro's effective use was limited to plus or minus 60 degrees in pitch, which at that time was adequate for most flight patterns. Of course, this would not be acceptable if one needed to know if one's wings were level throughout an Immelmann. This condition was essential to the maneuver that the Air Force and Navy wanted to use for their bomb-tossing scenario.

A very bright engineer at Wright-Patterson Air Force Base knew of our two-gyro platform work, and decided to fund an attempt to make our three-axis device provide unlimited freedom in all three axes. If this could be done, a pilot then could perform a complete loop and keep wings level by watching an indicator that showed pitch and roll through 360 degrees of pitch.

The attitude indicator, which already had been designed by my brother and his group, would have to be driven by what looked like signals from a *non-tumbling gyroscope*. There was no such thing!

That Wright-Patterson engineer, Max Lipscomb, went to our sales representative in Dayton. John Huff, our sales rep, and I had become friends from my earlier visits to Wright-Patterson, so he came to me with the problem and a proposal that we undertake the development contract.

We managed to win the contract. Because I had been involved in writing the proposal and had come to know Max, I was named project engineer and supervised an engineering and technical crew of six people. Today, such a project would probably be given one hundred people, each with his own computer.

My number one engineer was Ken Faux (pronounced as "fox"). We sat at adjacent desks in the bullpen at Lear. We would talk for hours about how to make the two-gyro platform look like a non-tumbling gyro.

Ken and I finally came up with the answer, with the help of some handmade gimbal models. It dawned on us that in vertical flight, a change in heading is a change in aircraft roll. In level flight, we controlled the outer roll gimbal from the inner roll gimbal signal.

However, in vertical fight we controlled the outer roll gimbal, which provided the roll or "wings level" signal to the attitude indicator or autopilot, from the azimuth (heading) signal provided by the directional gyro. To make the roll signal smooth, we mixed the inner roll signal with the azimuth signal through a sine-cosine resolver to control the roll gimbal.

Simple, huh? I'll skip the complicated part and just say that it worked. Ken and I got a U.S. patent for this invention, and the company gave each of us one dollar and a small plaque.

The company sold literally hundreds of millions of dollars' worth of Two-Gyro All Attitude Bombing systems to the Navy and Air Force.

Ken Faux and I worked together on many other projects over the subsequent years, and even got another patent. This one was a fore-aft accelerometer to cut off the gravity sensor during take-off. This would avoid allowing the vertical gyroscope to seek a false vertical reading and show incorrect data to the pilot about his take-off angle.

We called it a "fore-aft cut-off device." The Patent Office called it a Vertical Erection Device, so Ken and I never bragged much about it. Both patents noted the inventors to be Ken Faux, et al. I was the "et al.!"

During my stay at Lear from 1953 to 1965, my fortunes improved. I moved up in the organization, thanks to hard work and two higher-level mentors to whom I owe a great deal. One was Johanas (Hans) Thiry, the Vice President of Engineering at Lear during my entire tenure.

Hans was a German engineer who had worked at one time for the Siemens Company in Germany. During World War II, he reportedly worked with Dr. Werner Von Braun, the scientist who enabled the U.S. space program. He never talked about the war days to me, but he became a good friend and father figure to me. Hans was a wise, energetic, and entrepreneurial engineer.

My other champion was Joseph M. Walsh, who had come to the company as a financial officer in 1956. He soon became the assistant general manager, and then President and general manager of the Instrument Division.

Joe never bothered much with protocol or management levels, he got right to the point. He always would go directly to the person he trusted in the organization. Sometimes this behavior would put us in an awkward spot with our immediate supervisors; in my case, Hans!

Joe liked me and the feeling was mutual. One of the most important things Joe taught me was how to be pragmatic. Ultimately, Joe recommended me to Bill Lear to be part of the Lear Jet Team as the founder of Jet Electronics and Technology (JET), the aircraft instrument subsidiary of Lear Jet Industries.

Over this same period, my income rose to close to $20,000 per year, which was not bad in those days. There was also a small bonus at Christmas for a job well done, which was usually one to two thousand dollars.

Jeanette and I had bought our first house in 1954 for $12,250. It was a three-bedroom house with full basement, with 900 square feet on the main floor. It had no garage, but we managed to have one built in 1955. We bought that first home with a V.A. loan at four percent interest and a down payment from $25 bonds that we had saved in payroll deductions each month since 1950.

We even bought a brand new 1955 Plymouth coupe. Shortly afterwards, we became a *two car* family when I bought a 1950 Plymouth for driving to work.

In 1959, we moved to a bigger home in Cascade, Michigan, a small town ten miles east of Grand Rapids. We paid $19,000 for a three- bedroom house, which had close to 2,000 square feet with a large lawn, full basement and two-car garage, all in a lovely neighborhood.

Our next-door neighbor was the local pastor of the Cascade Christian Church, which we immediately joined. We became good friends with the Reverend Ray Gaylord and his wife, Jeannette.

Ray is without a doubt the most devout, practical, compassionate, and competent preacher I have ever known or heard of. The world would be a far better place if it were full of "Ray Gaylords."

In 1960, we added again to the baby boom when Sandra came along. Sand truly was the baby of the house, with fifteen year-old brother Johnny in high school, nine year-old brother Steve, and seven year-old sister Sue. She grew up in a much different environment than the rest of her family.

We were by then "upper middle-class America:" new cars, nice clothes, country club, Sunday dinner out at the best restaurants, and vacations to Arizona or Florida in winter, always with the family. All six of us would pile into the car and drive about 400 miles to our folks in Robinson. The kids loved it, and we had to scream at them only two or three times during the trip.

There were no freeways, no speed limits, no seat belts and I have a very heavy foot. How we avoided a serious accident I'll never know, except I've always been an alert driver and watched out for the other guy.

During the early 1960s, I advanced up the ranks in the engineering department to the position of Systems Engineering Division Manager, a big title and office. I was responsible for about 100 engineers who developed gyroscopes for military aircraft.

It was during this time that I had my first experiences in public speaking. I had to make many technical presentations to our customers, who included the government and private aircraft companies.

My first presentations were scary to me, to say the least. I came close to choking in those meetings, especially at big conferences. I soon became reasonably comfortable, partly from practice, but also due to the encouragement of one of our sales people who I consider to be one of my best friends.

This was John Huff, a tall, dark, pleasant fellow with a burr haircut, who possessed the highest degree of self-confidence I've ever seen in an individual. His self-confidence was interpreted by some people as arrogance, and women thought he was an absolute chauvinist.

John had a great sense of humor, and was one of those rare people who could tell a joke on himself and laugh as heartily as everyone else. I had the good fortune of sharing the podium with John at some of the conferences we attended.

I'll never forget one conference that took place in Palm Springs, California in 1962. It was the annual Air Force/industry symposium. All the military vendors and high-level Air Force procurement officers were there.

John and I made a joint presentation on a device called the "Geocentric Pendulum," a rather complicated instrument which supposedly improved the accuracy of determining the vertical reference for aircraft. It was a controversial project at Lear, with its sponsors being the "Advanced Engineers"—the group that most of us thought didn't contribute much to the success of the company.

Neither John nor I believed in the product, but we made a good presentation anyway. Before the presentation, John and I agreed that during the question and answer period, if a question stumped one of us, we would exchange glances. Somehow we would stall for enough time so that one of us would come up with an answer.

The first thing that happened was that a fellow from the Sperry Gyroscope Corporation got up and said: "I'm so and so from Sperry Gyroscope, and I'd like everyone here at this conference to know that we at Sperry tried this Geocentric thing ten years ago, and it didn't work. Mr. Huff, what do you say to that?"

I looked over at John. He had his back to me, and clearly intended that I answer this guy. The answer came to me in a flash.

I said, "I don't know about Sperry, but the state-of-the-art has improved at Lear in the last ten years!"

It brought the house down. The Sperry guy looked like an idiot, and Lear, Inc. gained more stature by that remark than with anything we had said or done in recent years.

This was especially pleasing to Bill Lear, who sat in the audience. He hated Sperry with a vengeance, because they seemed to have more recognition and influence.

On another occasion, one of our products was experiencing some serious failures. Out of the thousands of units we had shipped, several had malfunctioned.

I had set up a number of tests and determined the cause. We discovered it was possible that other failures could occur. It was clear that every unit needed to have major re-working done, in order to assure safety.

We were quick to notify the Air Force, because safety was always a primary concern at Lear. We informed the Air Force that every unit would need repair as soon as possible.

Our problem was how to minimize the cost. We had to find a way to have the Air Force pay for the correction.

I came up with a plausible, but almost tongue-in-cheek explanation of how we had properly designed the product to military specifications, but that these specifications were incomplete. The gaps in the specs allowed for the kind of failures we were experiencing.

This argument would stretch our credibility, but John Huff thought he could get our friends in the Air Force to support my position at a Board of Review headed by high-level Air Force officers. John and I went to this review, where I gave a presentation as to why the Air Force should pay us for correcting our own mistake.

When I finished my presentation, it was clear that John had done his job, because our Air Force civilian engineering friends immediately spoke up in support of my position.

It was very quiet in the room, a few muffled coughs and that was all. John, sensing that someone had to say something, decided to speak up. He said, "Gentlemen, in *collusion...*"

He meant to say "In *conclusion*," but it was too late. John himself burst out laughing, said, "*co-o-o-lusion*," and continued a genuine laugh aimed clearly at himself. The place broke up with laughter.

When it settled down, the senior officer thanked us. With a smile, he said, "I think the Air Force can manage a re-furbishment contract to your satisfaction."

Another memorable event involved an infamous presentation to a very high-level Pentagon contingent of admirals and generals.

Lear, Inc. had teamed up with IBM and Boeing Aircraft to bid on a ship-to-shore missile system. Lear was to build the guidance system, IBM the computer, and Boeing the missile itself.

All three of us contractors had practically forced the Pentagon to have a meeting. The senior officers had not wanted us, for they obviously already had made up their minds to give the contract to someone else. However, having used heavy political pressure, we were given an hour of their time.

When we arrived at the meeting room in the Pentagon, an admiral very curtly told us to make it fast, since he and his associates had *important* things to do.

I was up first and gave a 35 mm colored slide presentation on the Lear guidance system. It went very well and took about fifteen minutes.

The IBM guys were next and gave a paper flip chart presentation. The presentation went well, but I thought it was a little unprofessional because they didn't use slides.

The last person in our group was the Boeing project leader. He was a six foot, six inch tall man, with a sophisticated manner and the confidence of a real leader. Boeing was to be the lead contractor, so this guy was our big honcho. He was using colored slides.

Let me explain that the carousel projector had not been invented yet; we were using the straight magazine type of slide holder. We had balanced the projector on top of some telephone books on a stool. The magazine was loaded, and one of the Lear salesmen, a fellow named Mike Conlin, volunteered to run the projector. Years later, Mike took my place as President of Jet Electronics, and afterwards became President of Lear Jet.

When our Boeing leader said, "First slide, please," Mike hit the button. However, he hit "reverse" instead of "forward." The plastic cartridge containing 30 slides shot out the back of the projector, past the phone books and down to the floor with a bang.

The cartridge sprang open and slides shot everywhere. They actually fluttered like butterflies, covering probably 20 square feet of floor.

Panic!! Mike muttered something like, "My God!" Everyone, except our Boeing leader and the IBM guys, got on hands and knees trying to get the slides back in order and into the cartridge.

After ten minutes, we got everything back together and started the show again. The first slide was turned 90 degrees sideways, making the writing run vertically up the screen. Our Boeing leader calmly turned his head sideways, as did all of the admirals and generals, and proceeded with his presentation.

As may well be guessed, not one slide had been correctly inserted into the cartridge. There are eight ways to insert a slide into a cartridge, with seven of them wrong.

The coup-de-grace was the last slide. It was to depict the missile sailing elegantly into the sky from the ship towards the shore. Instead, the slide was upside down and depicted the missile going gracefully *underground* from ship to shore!

Never fear! Our leader went right on and calmly concluded the presentation.

In the end, the admirals and generals filed out of the room without comment: no smiles, no laughter, nothing. We looked at each other. The IBM presenter said, "The reason we at IBM use flip charts is to avoid such a disaster."

We didn't get the contract!

In the early 1960s, Bill Lear was devoting most of his time to commercial aviation in one way or another. His home was not far from the Lear, Inc. headquarters at the airport in Santa Monica.

The Lear-Cal Division was his primary interest. Lear-Cal made aircraft radios and commercial autopilots for private aircraft. The L-10 autopilot was very well liked by pilots, but the division never made significant profits. This was partly because Bill Lear meddled with the products, always changing something.

The Instrument Division in Grand Rapids was the big money-maker, pretty much because it was left undisturbed most of the time.

Bill wanted to design and build a business jet. He vigorously lobbied his Board of Directors, but to no avail. Some Board members thought he was irresponsible, and this "wild" idea certainly proved he was no businessman.

Bill solved this problem by selling his large and controlling interest in Lear to the Siegler company.

He took his approximately $10 million from the sale and went off to Switzerland to design and build the Lear Jet.

Why Switzerland? Because the Swiss government owned a fighter aircraft design which they had decided not to build. Instead, they had decided to buy the French Mirage, a simple make-or-buy decision.

Bill Lear knew a good thing when he saw it; he saw the Lear Jet in this abandoned Swiss fighter plane. He bought the rights from the Swiss government and modified it into the Lear Jet.

Now you know why the Lear Jet outperformed most of the world's jet fighters when it first came out.

The first Lear Jet didn't have a T-tail, where the horizontal stabilizer was on top of the vertical stabilizer. Instead, the horizontal stabilizer was half-way up the vertical stabilizer, much like the French Falcon.

Bill's intention to build the Lear Jet in Switzerland was soon abandoned. The Swiss culture and infrastructure just wasn't right from a practical standpoint. It certainly was not right for Bill Lear's way of doing things. You might work 25 or 30 hours straight through with Bill Lear, and Europeans stopped doing that shortly after the Industrial Revolution.

As a result, Bill moved the whole show in 1963, lock, stock, and barrel, to Wichita, Kansas, the heartland of U.S. commercial aviation.

Then Bill started building Lear Jets! They were new, shiny, all white, fully-equipped business jets, with a price tag of $449,000 each.

But were they truly *all new* business jets? The airframe and engines were new, but the instruments were government surplus!

Bill had gone to government bases and second-hand instrument dealers, and bought up all the old Lear gyros, autopilots and magnetic clutches he could find. He paid a few dollars per pound for this stuff, then overhauled it in a makeshift lab in the hangar in Wichita.

Bill was a shrewd and clever businessman, for which he received too little credit. He made Preston Tucker, the automobile magnate, look like a small-time operator.

IV

FLYING HIGH AND LOW

It was Halloween night in 1965, when I went to Bill Lear's home in Wichita to discuss something as yet unknown to me. I could tell that it was Halloween, because the witches were flying and Bill Lear was brewing up something.

I had received a very strange phone call on the previous day. It was a woman's voice, and all she said was: "Uncle Willy wants you to call him as soon as possible—today!"

I called Joe Walsh, who had left Lear-Siegler shortly after the sale of Lear, Inc., and asked him what Bill Lear wanted. That is when I learned that Bill had asked Joe who would be best to form an instrument division that would design and manufacture all of the instruments for the Lear Jet. Joe had recommended me.

Bill knew who I was, but we had not had much interaction in the twelve years I was at Lear, Inc. I knew his son, Bill Jr., better. During Bill Jr.'s few visits to Grand Rapids, we became friends. Bill Jr. was not a part of Lear Jet, so I did not consider the relationship important to my discussions with Bill Sr.

Bill Sr. never liked having to give up Lear, Inc., so he took his frustrations out on the Siegler people whenever he could. He saw in me a way to get all the talent that he needed to build another instrument concern, and get the quality instrument products he needed for the Lear Jet.

Bill wanted me to lease facilities in the Grand Rapids area, and hire all the people I needed to build a new instrument business. This business would supply Lear Jet, as well as other commercial and military customers.

Being eager and naive, and thinking of the "glory" of being a Vice President with Bill Lear's new company, I agreed to quit my Engineering Division manager's job at Lear-Siegler, and start the new Avionics Division of Lear Jet.

My salary was $25,000 per year, and I had options of $10 per share on 4000 shares of Bill's personal stock, which would vest in two years. At that time, those shares were trading on the public market for nearly $70 per share. To me, that stock couldn't go anywhere but up.

I resigned from Lear-Siegler the following Monday and caused quite a stir. Everyone was excited for me. Hans and Jim Bitner, the president, came to my going-away party.

I was a pretty popular guy at Lear, so the party was in the grand ballroom of the Pantlind Hotel, where the marquee had in lights, "Goodbye Johnny T." I hadn't told them I was staying in town!

My conscience wouldn't let me go through that evening without at least telling Bitner that I was going to form a new instrument company in town. That went over like throwing something awful in the punch bowl.

But no one else knew, so it was a great evening, with speeches from lots of folks, including my brother, Tom. Unfortunately, Tom was to suffer all the scorn that was to be dumped on me. This was justified somewhat, because I hired over 100 line people, engineers, and other professional people from the old company over the next few months.

I knew I had to have more than a design team to make a new business succeed reasonably fast. My intuition told me not to trust Bill Lear.

I was right! Bill had intended to keep the Lear Jet Avionics operation he already had in Wichita. After all, it was his first love.

During our Halloween night conversation, Bill made a casual response to a question about how difficult it might be to move the currently Wichita-based instrument operation to Grand Rapids. "Just back a truck up to the place, load it up, and it'll be done in two days."

About a month after I started to work for Lear Jet, I leased a 20,000 square foot factory in Grand Rapids and did exactly that. I had that division moved, and Bill didn't even know the trucks had been there.

Bill was furious. He called me in Grand Rapids, and asked who in the hell gave me the authority to move his instrument operation. I told him he did, and that he even told me how to do it, simply by backing up the trucks to the Wichita hangar and loading them up.

I told him I had people who knew more about that old equipment than anyone in Wichita. I had the people who built the original equipment, and invited him to come up to see a *real* instrument operation.

Bill refused to come to Grand Rapids, but he did something better. He sent his wife, Moya!

Moya Lear is a charming and outstanding lady. She is the daughter of Ole Olson, of "Hell's a Poppin'" fame, and a classy gal. We would never have tried to put anything over on her, *but* we put on a show of our operation, with photographers and press interviews on the front page of the local papers.

Moya stole the show, and went back to Wichita with front page pictures of herself, Jeanette, and me. Moreover, she had honest reports for Bill on what a smart thing he had done in starting the Lear Jet Avionics business in Grand Rapids.

Bill was the talk of the town, and I was nominated by the Greater Grand Rapids Chamber of Commerce for Man of the Year in 1965. Bill Lear was a clever old fox, but I was no fool.

Bill was an intimidating person. He kept people around him to carry his briefcase or perform menial tasks. Not me! The first time he ordered me to do some trivial duty, I refused! He just smiled and never asked me again.

This is not to say that he didn't get mad at me or occasionally fire me. More on that later.

Bill's background was the quintessential Horatio Alger story. He had less than a high school education, but his flair for the spectacular and his absolute genius for electronics, especially radio, had led him to become the co-founder of Motorola with Robert Galvin in the 1920s. He sold his share of Motorola to Galvin in order to pursue other interests.

Bill later got involved with General Sarnoff of RCA, when he invented a major breakthrough component for radio that was something RCA unsuccessfully had been trying to do for years. Bill Lear received significant compensation for this effort.

By the time he started his own businesses, Bill had established close ties at the top levels in RCA and Motorola.

Shortly after the visit from Moya, I was in Wichita to visit my number one "customer." Bill had decided that he, Moya, and an entourage would journey to Grand Rapids for a two-day visit. We would take his personal Lear Jet and arrive at 5:00 p.m. in Grand Rapids.

That trip was memorable for a number of reasons.

On the way to Grand Rapids, at 41,000 feet in altitude, Bill pulled the autopilot amplifier from under his seat; he was always the pilot.

Bill had installed the amplifier with an extra long cable so he could put it on his lap. There, he could get at the pitch and roll gain potentiometers, or "pots", with a small shirt-pocket screw driver.

A quick turn of the roll pot would result in something close to a snap roll. The same adjustment on the pitch pot would put you into a sickening zero-gravity dive.

Bill would make these adjustments for two reasons. He wanted to get a feel for the autopilot response, and he wanted to scare the hell out of unsuspecting passengers. He accomplished the latter, for sure.

This trip was also my first exposure to the showmanship of the famous William P. Lear, Sr.

We were scheduled to land at about 5:00 p.m. in Grand Rapids. It was a clear but cold December day. On the previous day, there had been a heavy snowstorm, making the runways snow-packed and slippery.

The early Lear Jets didn't have thrust reversers, so that braking was the only way to decelerate. No problem! One of the innovative systems on this Lear Jet was an anti-skid brake system which worked perfectly that day, as always. These anti-skid systems are now available 20 years later on luxury autos.

We came to a safe landing in Grand Rapids, and taxied up to the glare of lights, cameras, and dozens of press, TV photographers, and writers. Bill always made sure that he was photographed in the pilot's seat, big smile and all.

The rest of the entourage got out: Mrs. Lear, Ed Chandler (the V.P. of aircraft sales), a couple of Bill's cronies, and me. Also on the flight was the co-pilot, who was almost left behind in Wichita because he hadn't been watching Bill's office door to see when Bill rushed out to the plane.

Moya, of course, was immediately recognized by the press, so she was inundated with questions. But the real prize was Bill Lear himself. When he deplaned, the crowd cheered, and the photographers and reporters had a field day.

Bill introduced me and told the press how we would employ thousands of people (we had 15 on staff at that time), and generate millions of dollars of revenue in the next few years. He talked about things such as new factories and improved facilities at the airport, which included longer runways and new electronic breakthroughs.

It was a grand show. The press loved it! It was like a homecoming, since it was the first time Bill Lear had been in Grand Rapids after he had sold Lear, Inc. several years previously. The town loved him because he brought excitement. They thought: he had built a business there once before, why not a second time?

We had a dinner that night at the best steakhouse in town. Jeanette sat next to Bill, who charmed her to pieces. All in all, it was a memorable day.

The next morning, I picked up the Lears in my new 1965 Buick Electra and we spent the day at the factory. Bill was pleased with the production line, where we were overhauling the old autopilot equipment and shipping it to Wichita to be put in Lear Jets.

He was fascinated with my engineering staff, especially John Jessup, who had all kinds of innovative ideas on new kinds of gyroscopes (for example, one made of fiber-filled epoxy) and other products. Bill was so pleased with what he saw that he told me to plan on moving to new and larger facilities at the Kent County airport.

Bill instructed me to quietly acquire property along the east-west runway and lay out plans for new instrument manufacturing facilities. I also was to plan for a hangar for Lear Jets, including one for my division. We even made preliminary plans to install instruments and radios into Lear Jets in a Grand Rapids facility.

One could say that we were looking pretty good for a little start-up division of Lear Jet.

I was concerned, however, that we were completely captive as a supplier to Lear Jet's aircraft division. I knew this new business must acquire more customers if it were to be successful. "Pseudo-profits" are fine if everyone does well, but there's nothing like bringing *real* money into the corporation.

My first thought was to try to license a product I had seen when I was at Lear-Siegler. It was developed and made in small quantities by a French instrument company located in Paris, called SFENA.

The Air Force at Wright-Patterson Field had for some time wanted a small, standby attitude indicator that could operate on battery power in an emergency. This was important in addressing a problem with jet aircraft.

Because jet aircraft have substantially higher speeds and sensitive control characteristics, they cannot be flown "by the seat of the pants." Instrument flying requires more than "needle, ball, and airspeed" to keep the plane in a flyable and safe attitude.

All jets, of course, had the standard three-inch or five-inch two-axis attitude indicator for pitch and roll altitude. However, these instruments were driven by a remote vertical gyroscope, and both the gyro and indicator were driven by the ship's power.

If you lost electrical power during bad weather, you literally could not fly the airplane. This is why the military was interested in an attitude indicator which could operate from battery power, or could operate for a few minutes with no power at all.

I had seen the SFENA self-contained unit while at Lear-Siegler, and had tried to get that company to license the unit from the French. No way!

Lear-Siegler considered itself the authority on aircraft instruments, and would not stoop to use someone else's design. Moreover, the gyroscope was inside the indicator container and actually was geared to the ball. A purist knows that gyroscopes don't perform their best when subjected to the friction generated by these gears. So, Lear-Siegler turned thumbs down on the SFENA unit.

I got on an airplane with an old associate named Pete Peterson, and we headed for Paris. Pete had been a consultant to Lear and now represented SFENA in the U.S. When we got to Paris, I met with the head of SFENA's production and engineering, a very pleasant gentleman in his 50s.

Pete and I spent all day trying to convince him that my new little start-up operation could build his unit in the U.S. We had dinner at his apartment in Paris that night, and met his lovely wife and daughter. It was a delightful evening and concluded with our host telling us he would arrange for a meeting with the president of SFENA on the following day.

At the meeting with the president on the following morning, we were met with courtesy. To our dismay, we were told by the president that he personally had made a handshake deal with a senior vice president of the Bendix Corporation to have that company build the standby indicator in the U.S.

The deal had been made on the previous day, and the Bendix vice president was heading home to get approval from his management. The only problem had been that SFENA wanted the unit made to metric specifications. Bendix wanted to respecify and make the necessary changes in order to build the unit in standard English decimal units.

I should have been a salesman! I made the best presentation of why Lear Jet Avionics should be the licensee for the SFENA product. I convinced the president that it would get "lost" in Bendix, but in my shop it would have my personal attention.

I concluded by telling him that we would build the unit to metric specs. Furthermore, I would sign the deal right then because I didn't need anyone else's approval. I knew Bill Lear would approve the deal. We signed the agreement that afternoon and I went home with a new product.

We built the unit and obtained approval to sell it to the Air Force. It became standard equipment on all U.S. military aircraft. To this day, 23 years later, it is still the military standard as well as being used now on most commercial aircraft.

On a recent trip with my fifteen year-old grandson, we toured a B-1 bomber. I noticed my little standby indicator right in the center of the instrument panel.

When I mentioned to the pilot that I was responsible for that instrument being in military aircraft, he looked at me and said, "Mr. Titsworth, you saved my life last week!" Now, that's *real* reward for entrepreneurship.

Besides getting an airplane designed and in production after moving the company from Switzerland to Wichita, and starting a new division in Grand Rapids with me, Bill Lear had *in his spare time*, invented the 8-track stereo music system!

In California, "Madman" Muntz had invented the 4-track stereo. Bill made an 8-track unit *and* made it work with clever, innovative features.

Bill always had an interest in the music business, ever since his early radio days when he was a co-founder of Motorola. His close ties to RCA and "the General" came from his early work in radio. It therefore was not surprising to those who knew him to see him working on another new approach to music, especially something for the automobile.

The 8-track tape stereo system for automobiles was truly a marvelous product. The after-market, with its large distribution system, went absolutely bananas over it.

"After-market" is a term that describes when products, such as radios, are sold for installation in cars already purchased by the owner. This is in contrast to selling directly from our factory to a car manufacturer for original installation.

With speakers in the doors of a Cadillac, your favorite music on 8-track endless tape (no re-wind), and with good stereo amplifiers, you would think you had "died and gone to heaven!"

Bill Lear wanted to go after the big boys in Detroit: Chrysler, General Motors, and Ford. In 1965, he wanted his unit in every 1966 automobile.

The fact that the auto companies typically would take two years to plan a new accessory like this didn't bother William P. Lear. After all, it only took him three months to *invent*, *design* and *build* the first model.

Never mind that Sam Auld, his most trusted technical brain, hadn't slept for weeks.

One day in 1965, Bill took his sample, walked into Ford headquarters and demonstrated his amazing product. When he said he wanted to put the unit in the 1966 model cars, the Ford executives had to come up with something besides: "there's not enough time."

They told him it looked fine, but they really needed something that was smaller, so it could fit where the radio goes. By the way, it had to have a radio in it as well.

Bill said he'd be back in 30 days. In one month, he came back with a unit that fit in the radio slot, *and* it had an FM radio in it!

This time, the Ford people had to find a real stopper. They said that Lear Jet didn't have a factory close to Detroit, so they wouldn't buy the product. But, if Lear would give Motorola a license, Ford could buy from them.

Bill Lear gave Motorola a license, leased a building from Motorola that was located in Detroit, and went into production on his own 8-track stereo unit.

Back in Grand Rapids, the Avionics Division was a successfully growing operation by mid-1966. Lear Jet was booming! We won the "Bull of the Year" award from Wall Street in 1965, and our public over-the-counter stock was selling at around $80 per share.

My options were at $10 per share, so I was a cinch to be worth $250,000 in another year or so. Understand that my net worth at that time from other assets was probably less than $10,000, so we're talking *big* money.

The Avionics Division provided static power supplies, attitude indicators, anti-skid systems, autopilots, an altitude warning system, and various other instruments for the model 23 and 24 Lear Jets.

We also had landed a contract with the Air Force for the small standby attitude indicator for fighter aircraft. This was the unit I had licensed from SFENA, the French instrument maker.

It was time to look for a larger, permanent facility for the Avionics Division. I started a study of land sites, and found that a young man in town had control of 150 acres adjacent to the Kent County airport along the east-west runway. We could buy the land for less than $1000 per acre.

The owner had given a fellow named Van Gimmert an option to buy the land, and he in turn was trying to sell it for a quick profit. I had not known about this arrangement. All I knew was that it was a prime location, and I didn't want someone else to snap it up. We negotiated with Van Gimmert through a broker and acquired the property.

Years later, after I joined Xerox, they sent a plane to Minneapolis to pick up Jeanette and me. The Xerox chief pilot flew the company jet that day, and during the flight back to New York he introduced himself, saying, "Do you remember me? I'm Dick Van Gimmert, the fellow you bought the Kent County Airport property from in 1966."

We had a great conversation about that and other events in Grand Rapids. Dick told me his option had one more day to go when we had agreed to buy the land. The next day, we could have bought it for much less. Of course, 20 years later it was worth 20 times what we had paid for it.

Having acquired the land, I hired an architect to draw a rendering of the new 60,000 square foot facility and design a plant layout. We worked several months on the plans for this new building. When we had the cost estimate, which as I recall was less than $3 million, I sent the plans to Bill Lear. I asked for what I assumed would be routine approval.

The plans came back in about three days, approved! However, there was a note on the margin: *"Build it underground."*

Well, that was typical Bill Lear! It wasn't a joke, for he was serious. Bill felt this would save money on heating and air conditioning, and improve efficiency, since there would be no windows for the employees to look through.

There was no alternative but make a study of how to build this facility underground. My architect quit on the spot. I couldn't find anyone in Michigan who had ever done something like this, so we started looking around the country and the world.

We found a bank in Chicago which had built its data center underground for security reasons. They had a hard time getting employees to work there, but fortunately they didn't need many. We also went to Sweden, where SAAB had built several plants under a mountain.

One of the things that people overlook in underground facilities is that you don't save as much as you think on heating and air conditioning, because the air must be exchanged continuously. The air comes from above ground, and has to be heated or cooled just as it would be in a conventional building.

That didn't matter to Bill Lear; he wanted the building underground!

I couldn't find a contractor who would consider such a project. I finally got one to do some soil tests. He found that the water table was very high at our site. There was just a slight wink of his eye when he reported that to me.

It seemed that pumps would have to be run continuously to prevent flooding. In the event the building lost power, the plant would be flooded. That discovery prompted Bill to reluctantly change his view, and we got approval to proceed as originally planned.

The business in Grand Rapids was becoming so interesting that Bill started to stop in occasionally. There would be no notice of a visit, except for a call from the airport saying that Mr. Lear was over Chicago in his Lear Jet, and would be landing in 20 minutes. This was just enough time for me to get to the airport to pick him up.

A Bill Lear plant visit was always eventful. The press was usually notified and eager for a story from Bill. They usually got one.

One time Bill told them about plans on digitizing humans and transporting them across telephone lines in seconds. They loved it.

He was always telling them about plans for new products, and about new airplanes that were not yet on the drawing boards. Our public relations and legal people were continuously in a state of shock, since he was treading on dangerous ground with the Securities and Exchange Commission.

Bill and I once addressed the Association of Security Analysts in New York at a time when we were making a second public offering of stock. We rehearsed the evening before with carefully written scripts to avoid any improper disclosures during this sensitive period.

During my presentation, I delivered my pitch word for word.

Bill started to read his speech, when he suddenly looked up at his audience and said: "This is a lot of bull. Let me tell you what's really going on."

With that, he threw his several loose pages of script out toward the audience. Bill exuberantly told them all about the new wonderful things we were going to do, all the while making extremely optimistic projections of revenues and profits.

I thought our legal counsel was going to die.

Bill got away with it. That was the year our stock got the "Bull of the Year" award. It seemed things couldn't be better.

The first thing that Bill Lear usually would do after he arrived at the Grand Rapids airport would be to chew on me all the way from the airport to the plant. He always complained about how lousy the autopilot was on his airplane.

On the way from Wichita, Bill would make several "adjustments" by resetting the trim potentiometer. As I have described previously, this would involve putting the aircraft through sudden dives and rolls. I pitied his poor passengers.

To duplicate Bill's "fine tuning," we were supposed to do such things as re-wire the unit to make it more responsive or put in a delay circuit. As Bill would be at the plant for two hours, he thought that was plenty of time to remove the autopilot and re-wire it!

The first couple of times Bill came in, that was exactly what we did. While my engineers were frantically rebuilding the autopilot, he would wander through the factory, changing processes and products at will, and generally creating havoc.

Bill didn't care that one could lose control of product changes or design, and get into trouble with the Federal Aviation Administration. That was *my* problem.

The engineers would tell me each time that there was nothing wrong with the autopilot, and that if Mr. Lear would simply leave the adjustments alone, everything would be OK.

So, I got an idea. I told the engineers just to set the pots back to nominal; that is, their original settings.

We started doing that instead of re-wiring the units. Bill would come to town, go through his tirade about the lousy autopilot and that we didn't understand the design, and then give us the usual instructions. We ignored him and set the adjustable pots back to where they belonged.

Bill would fly away and always call in to the office from his plane, saying, "Now that's a *real* autopilot."

We all knew that the "old man" had a good sense of humor. At the next Christmas, we gave him a shirtpocket screwdriver with a loose handle, and told him what we had been doing. He laughed as hard as any of us.

Another idea I had was how to keep Bill out of my factories. Some of my colleagues had tried to keep him out by telling their people not to take orders from him. The result was that my colleagues inevitably got fired, because Bill was the boss and he made sure everyone knew it.

I knew better than to try that dumb stunt. Instead, I would have a little talk with my engineers before Bill would arrive. I would tell them to think up every new idea they could, no matter how far-fetched.

On the way to the plant from the airport, I would tell Bill that my engineers had a number of new things cooking. Would he spend some time with them?

Bill would be completely absorbed in his conversations with my engineers, with no time to visit the shop floor. He loved it, and so did the engineers. In fact, some good ideas came from those sessions.

There is no doubt that Bill Lear was a real genius. He turned many of his original ideas into products, but he also "borrowed" many ideas as well. He could see someone else's idea and find a practical way to produce it.

Bill surrounded himself with bright people who could take direction. He would turn them loose on somebody else's idea and before you knew it, Bill had another "invention."

He didn't steal ideas, he simply made them work; something the originator didn't know how to do. That's a great talent, and takes nothing away from Bill Lear's genius.

Perhaps his two greatest contributions were not his own inventions. One was the 8-track stereo music system and the other was the Lear Jet aircraft.

In the fall of 1966, things started to falter in the company whose name had been changed from Lear Jet, Inc. to Lear Jet Industries.

Over several months in early 1966, we had lost some aircraft in dramatic crashes. As I recall, two had made uncontrolled power dives at nearly the speed of sound. There was nothing left but deep holes. Another had flown into a mountain in Palm Springs.

There was no clue as to the nature of the problem. As always, there was endless speculation about structural problems with the airplane.

Finding the cause of airplane accidents is a long and tedious process. It was clearly going to take many months to find out anything.

We were afraid that the FAA would ground the plane, which would put us out of business. As it turned out, they didn't have to ground the plane to ruin the company. We managed to do that by ourselves.

With the uncertainty of the aircraft's safety, our market dried up. That alone might not have ruined us, but Bill Lear, ever the optimist, was sure that nothing was wrong with the aircraft.

He used up our available cash to buy hundreds of jet engines and other extremely expensive parts. These parts were required to continue production at the high rate we were enjoying before the accidents occurred.

We were running out of cash!

To add to the problem, the Stereo Division in Detroit was having great difficulties in making shipments. It also had quality problems with the products that were shipped.

The plant had been equipped and production had started in less than three months from the time the 8-track stereo was demonstrated to Ford. Orders were rolling in and the backlog was very large.

Ninety percent of the orders were from dealers and distributors in the after-market. These dealers saw the 8-track stereo as the greatest product they had ever seen and were clamoring for units.

Their problem was that they couldn't get enough units quickly. Moreover, about 30 percent of the units they did get failed to operate properly, so they sent them back to the Lear Jet Stereo factory.

Part of our problem was that distributors and dealers typically don't pay their bills early. In fact, most of them will wait until *they* are paid before they pay you.

Here was another cash flow problem, aggravated by the high percentage of returned goods.

The only division of the company that was doing reasonably well was my little Avionics Division. Our arms'-length transactions with the Aircraft Division and our Air Force and Navy contracts were paying well. As a result, we were making nice profits.

However, we were too small to have much of a financial impact on Lear Jet Industries. The Aircraft Division was still our largest customer; if they got into real trouble, my division would also have problems.

In October, 1966, Bill called and asked if I would do him a big favor by taking over the Stereo Division. He suggested that I could commute from Grand Rapids to Detroit, which was "only" a three hour drive.

I could also retain my position as head of the Avionics Division, where we could assign someone temporarily to run that operation while I was "cleaning up" the Stereo Division.

Having been trained all my life to do what I was asked, I took the assignment. I gave Mike Conlin, our marketing/sales manager, the temporary general manager job at Avionics.

I took people from my operation with me to Detroit. They included: the head of manufacturing, Al Brizzalaro, the head of personnel, George Brooks, and Bob Eddy, my chief financial officer. We "commuted" weekly, staying in a Howard Johnson's motel during the week.

What we found in Detroit was an unbelievable mess. Several models of the 8-track stereo had been put into production much too quickly. There were big design and manufacturing process problems, which resulted in terrible product quality. No wonder 30 percent were coming back!

But that was just the beginning.

Because of the numerous and continuous design changes, most of the parts inventory was useless. There were no financial reserves for bad inventory.

Then, a bigger problem was uncovered.

Bob Eddy and Al Brizzalaro came into the office one day and said, "Guess what we found over on Eight Mile Road?"

It was a rented warehouse, full of thousands of returned stereo players.

These stereos all had been shipped to customers and declared as revenue, but had not been counted against revenue when they were returned. Of course, they had never been paid for by the customer.

Besides the obvious cash problem, we had a big profit and loss headache. Apparently, the previous general manager and financial officer had intended to repair and ship back each returned unit within a month. This would ensure that all that would hit the books would be the repair costs.

But, they couldn't keep up the repairs on time. They also were afraid to tell "Uncle Willy" what had happened.

I can't recall the amount of the write-off we took that first month, but it was several millions of dollars. To make matters worse, we needed cash to buy new inventory and properly tool the production lines.

The management situation was very interesting, to say the least. The production workforce of about 500 people was 95 percent women. All of them were black and members of the Teamsters' union.

This was in 1966 and 1967, when the country was at a peak in racial unrest. The Detroit riots had occurred in early 1967, and our factory was very close to the center of the riot area.

Perhaps because we employed so many blacks, and I'd like to think because I've always had great respect for our employees and treated them fairly, we didn't have so much as a broken window.

The people indeed were good workers. It certainly wasn't their fault that the company wasn't doing well.

The union didn't seem to care about much except collecting their dues, so I didn't have a problem there. It was simply a matter of debugging the designs and getting some consistent manufacturing processes in place.

This took far more time than Bill Lear thought it should.

He was always flying in unannounced and "helping" us with our production and quality problems.

One time, shortly after I had taken over, Bill came to the factory. After a few minutes in the production area, he stormed into my office and said: "There are too many people in the production area. By tomorrow morning I want the number reduced by 50 percent!"

It was four o'clock in the afternoon when he gave me that order. The next morning, when nothing had happened, he looked me straight in the eye and stated that I had better have a damned good explanation as to why I hadn't laid off half of the workforce.

I said, "Bill, with no more time than you gave me, there was a good chance I would have laid off the wrong half."

He was quiet for a while, then burst out laughing and said, "OK, take a few days, but cut down the size of that workforce!"

He was absolutely correct, and we did cut back significantly, although it was not 50 percent.

Another time, Bill stopped in for a few hours on his way from Wichita to New York. When I met the plane, he and Moya got out of the plane, followed by a young priest.

I wondered why Bill Lear would have a priest with him, since he himself thought he was God.

We all went to the factory together. As we entered, Bill said, "Johnny, take the Father to your office and buy him a cup of coffee while I go through the production area." The last thing I wanted was for Bill to go through the factory alone, but I had little choice but to be courteous to the young priest.

In my office, over coffee, I asked the priest how he came to know the Lears. He said he didn't know them at all; he had been on a tour of the aircraft plant with some of his parishioners, when the guide said, "Father, would you like to meet Mr. Lear?"

The Father thought that would be nice, and to his delight he soon met both Mr. and Mrs. Lear as they were walking towards the flight line. Bill asked him if he'd like a ride in a Lear Jet. Of course, the good Father agreed.

The priest was looking around rather nervously in my office and said: "We're in Detroit—I thought we were just going to fly around Wichita for a few minutes and land. The members of my parish will be looking for me. Do you know what time the Lears are going back to Wichita?"

I said, "Father, I'm sorry but the Lears aren't going back to Wichita today. They're on their way to New York City."

The last time I saw the good Father, he was waving goodbye on his way to New York.

Bill Lear delighted in practical jokes and putting people in their place. He didn't like pretentious people or those who thought themselves important or too good for others.

When visiting Detroit with some high-level stuffed shirt, one of his favorite tricks was to say to me, in front of our guest: "Johnny, don't you think we should take so-and-so to the Waldorf for lunch?"

I knew he meant the little bar down the street, so we would head over there, while our guest was expecting the best.

This place would all but gag a maggot. We'd go in the rear entrance next to the "john," which you couldn't miss. The entrance was a torn screen door. Inside was a bar with a small grill, a few bare tables, and a pool table.

The bartender knew us and he would let Bill grill the hamburgers, which was one of his favorite pastimes. We would eat hamburgers and drink beer, while brushing away the flies.

The look on our guest's face would make Bill's day.

By late 1966, things were getting desperate for Lear Jet Industries. We weren't selling airplanes, the Stereo Division was struggling, and the Avionics Division needed cash to meet its growing orders.

It was during this period in my management career that I learned that no problem in a company is as big as limited or no cash.

For months I had not been able to pay Stereo Division creditors except partial or token payments. We were so far behind that our suppliers were personally calling me.

The verbal abuse was almost more than I could handle. I was harassed so much that I developed a twitch in my left eye. I would try to look casual by holding my hand to the side of my head to hide this affliction. I was becoming a 40 year-old basket case.

We had two creditors threatening involuntary bankruptcy, and it only takes three to have the courts declare you bankrupt.

I had my chief financial officer withdraw the cash from our account and put it in the company safe. I was afraid someone would garnish the account, making me unable to meet the payroll.

I never forgot those trying times, both from a personal and business standpoint. The emotional strain was hard, as I had been away from my family for a year, except for weekends.

My health was being affected. I had stomach problems from stress, lousy restaurant food, and too much booze. Fortunately, I did not become addicted to alcohol, as some of my associates did.

I decided the job wasn't worth the misery, and would have left the company had it not been sold.

From a business view, I learned that the most critical factor to running a business is cash flow.

There is no problem more serious than to run out of cash. Every manager, especially in large corporations, should be trained in cash management.

Late in 1966, the Board of Directors for Lear Jet Industries convinced Bill that he had to sell the company to save it.

In the meantime, Bill and Moya had put up for sale all of their personal holdings, including an old Master's painting and their private home in Wichita.

The company was broke, and so were the Lears.

During the fall of 1966, we had somehow held things together. The stock value had dropped from $80 per share to less than $10 per share. We were all very short-tempered, and at times a little irrational.

My sales manager was a typically optimistic salesman and showed very little concern or understanding of the cash problem. He kept making deals we couldn't afford, such as orders that would require extra cash.

I fired him, which was clearly a mistake on my part. He was very well-liked by our customers, and was probably all that kept many of them loyal.

With brother Tom,
1930.

With Mom
and brother Tom,
1931.

High school days, 1942.

With brother Tom, 1932.

The aviation cadet, 1943.

Engaged to Jeanette,
1945.

In college at Rose-Poly, 1946.

Starting at Lear Jet Avionics, 1965.

Bill Lear
tells another story,
1965.

Returning to Grand Rapids: (*left to right*) Bill and Moya Lear, Ed Chandler, me, and copilots, 1965.

Mom and Dad on their fiftieth anniversary, 1975.

Home in New Canaan, 1980.

Brother Tom, 1987.

With my Mom, 1981.

Jeanette, me, and our children, Steven (*top*), Susan (*center*), Sandra, and John, 1987.

With brother Joe (*left*) and Lloyd Thorndyke (*center*), 1990.

Chairman of the Board, Rose-Hulman Institute of Technology, 1990.

I even got fired myself. One morning, I was having a staff meeting in my office, when my secretary buzzed me and said that Mr. Lear was on the phone.

I put him on the speaker phone, which I hate for people to do to me, but at the time I didn't care.

Bill said, in an angry voice that we all could hear: "I've figured out what's wrong with the Stereo Division."

I said, "Fine, would you mind telling me?"

He said, "It's the God-damned management."

I said, "I'm the management."

He said, "I know who the management is!" and then he slammed the phone down.

I hung up and calmly went on with my meeting, even though my staff was in a state of shock. A few minutes later, my secretary announced that Mr. Lear was on the phone again.

I put him on the speaker phone again, and he said in a very pleasant tone, "Johnny, I just wanted to call you and tell you what a fine job you're doing up there in Detroit." Then he hung up.

I guess it dawned on him that if I left, he didn't have anyone who would take such a lousy assignment.

In January, 1967, it was clear that the company was going under. I had less than a month's cash for payroll in both the Avionics and Stereo Divisions, and the Aircraft Division was just as bad.

The good old days were gone. It wasn't fun anymore as it was when Uncle Willy would come to town. Back then, we would all work until the wee hours, find a bar somewhere, have a few drinks, and tell jokes.

Have you ever wondered who thinks up jokes? I'd swear it was Bill Lear. He would tell a bunch of new jokes every time he came to town. Some of them were pretty raw, but because of the way he told them, they were funny as hell.

Bill had a quick wit. When some stuffed shirt had complained about not being able to stand up in a Lear Jet and wondered why there was no toilet, Bill had calmly replied, "This plane is so fast you can go anywhere in less than three hours. You travel that long in your Cadillac and you don't stand up in it. And I never heard of anybody taking a crap in a Cadillac."

Shortly after the first of the year, there were several companies showing interest in buying Lear Jet. One was the Ling-Tempo-Vought Corporation (LTV).

As it turned out, Bill asked me to escort the executive from LTV through the Avionics and Stereo operations. I was to pick him up in Chicago in a Lear Jet, fly him to Grand Rapids and then to Detroit.

When I met him in Chicago, he was rude and arrogant, and kept making disparaging remarks about the airplane. He kept referring to it as a "kiddy-car." Hank Baird, our chief test pilot, was our pilot that day. I told Hank to give the guy a "real" ride.

I don't know what our climb-out angle was, but for sure, no one was going to get out of his seat. We did everything on the way to Grand Rapids but barrel rolls. It had to be the ride of the LTV executive's life.

He was very quiet after that, but showed very little interest in our company.

The serious suitor turned out to be Charlie Gates, of the Gates Rubber Company in Denver.

Charlie was in his late 40s and owned Gates Rubber, one of the largest privately-held companies in the U.S. He was an airplane buff and an experienced jet pilot.

Gates owned Comb's Aviation, a fixed base operator with a number of installations around the Midwest. A "fixed base operator" is a company that sells private aircraft and services for private aircraft, such as fuel, at major airports.

I'm not sure why Gates wanted Lear Jet. A consulting firm had done a study for him, and recommended that his company expand into transportation.

I think Charlie used that as an excuse to buy Lear Jet, but his real reason was that he was in love with aviation. There was something exciting about owning Lear Jet. Making fan belts isn't the most glamorous business in the world.

All you had to do was *work* for Lear Jet to get attention. Lear Jet was the "talk of the town," the "American dream," the last real swashbuckling institution around. Bill Lear was Howard Hughes, Preston Tucker, and George Patton all rolled into one.

Even in those desperate days, Bill Lear didn't lose his cool. He called me one evening in Detroit to tell me that the deal was off with Gates.

It seemed that Charlie not only wanted all of Bill's personally owned shares, but he didn't want recently promised options to be issued to employees.

Bill had promised each of my officers in Avionics and Stereo modest stock options for their loyalty. As I recall, the total was less than 50,000 shares, but none of the promises were on paper.

When Charlie Gates insisted that these options were not to be issued, Bill told him to go to hell. I urged Bill to forget about the options and told him that not a single officer would object.

We were flat "busted." I wasn't going to make the payroll the following week. Bill Lear was going to personally receive about $22 million for the sale of the company, and the rest of us would keep our jobs if the Gates deal was closed.

But Lear didn't budge.

Charlie Gates came back in a few days and the deal was closed. We all got our options, although, at least in my case, they never paid.

A few days afterwards, Jeanette and I met for dinner with Mr. and Mrs. Gates and Mr. and Mrs. Lear in Grand Rapids. Charlie casually asked me how much money we needed in Detroit the following week. He was a little surprised when I said $3 million would quiet our creditors and cover payroll.

Two days later, when I got back to Detroit, my chief financial officer said the bank called to tell him that a deposit of $3 million had been made in our account. He couldn't believe it. Neither could our creditors, who were all paid.

I soon learned that there is no such thing as a "friendly take-over." I ended up being the only surviving senior officer of Lear Jet.

The Gates company dismissed every one except me, and in my case, it wasn't because of my talent or personal character. It was because Avionics was relatively small and the Gates Company didn't know anything about the aircraft instrument business.

They considered themselves experts in the aircraft business and the stereo music business, the latter because it was a commodity business, like the tire and fan belt business. I tried to explain that the music products business was different, mostly because the Japanese were becoming serious competitors.

One of the things we had done in the Stereo Division was to make a tentative license deal with Matsushita to produce 50,000 units each month. They could ship a stereo player to Detroit at a full cost of $18 per unit, compared to our cost of over $30 per unit, and the quality was superior.

I wrote a report to Charlie urging him to conclude this deal and get out of the manufacturing part of the music business. He could make his money from the design and distribution of products.

The Gates organization completely ignored me and canceled the Japanese deal. Five years later, the Stereo operation went out of business, having lost it all to the Japanese.

I went back to Grand Rapids to run the Avionics business, which was prospering and never had a loss quarter since we started it.

Twenty years after the Avionics business was started, it was a $60 million operation. This was far more than the price Gates paid for all of Lear Jet. Gates sold the Avionics division to the Goodrich Rubber Company. Gates previously had changed the name of the business to Jet Electronics and Technology (JET). Currently, JET is still a going concern.

If I had known in 1967 what I know now about business, I would have found financial backing and bought the Avionics business.

Without Bill Lear, the company was never the same. Although Charlie Gates was a competent businessman, he was no Bill Lear.

The excitement and fun were gone. The bureaucracy of the old Gates Rubber Company soon took over. My new plant, which was on hold during 1966, was postponed indefinitely by Gates.

It was time to think about moving on.

As luck would have it, I found an opportunity at Control Data.

V

MANAGING SUCCESS
AT CDC

It's strange sometimes how opportunities arise. One arose for me as a result of a conversation I had with Bill Lear in 1967, after he had moved to Reno to work on his steam turbine engine.

Bill still had his personal Lear Jet and needed a directional gyro. He called me to get it free of charge. He never paid full price for anything.

I told him that the Gates people had me tied up in knots in that regard, and that I had to quote him a list price on equipment. Bill was furious and said he would go to Collins Radio. I told him Collins used rebuilt Sperry gyros, which I knew he wouldn't want.

After he told me I didn't know what I was talking about, I decided to at least prove it to myself. I called Collins to talk to an acquaintance from earlier Lear days, a fellow named G.G. "Gerry" Smith.

It seemed Gerry had gone to the Control Data Corporation (CDC), so I called CDC in Minneapolis. The switchboard operator wanted to know which Gerry Smith I wanted: the industrial engineer or the general manager of the Normandale

Disk Division. I said the industrial engineer, because that's what Gerry was when I knew him at Lear.

It turned out instead that he was the general manager. When I reached Gerry, he confirmed my understanding about the Sperry gyroscopes, but then he asked me how I liked working for Gates. I told him it was fine, but it was nothing like the old days.

Gerry said CDC was booming and there were many Lear guys there, including Thomas G. Kamp, who was Gerry's boss and number two to W.C. "Bill" Norris, the president of CDC.

Gerry said that I should move to CDC. He also said that if I would take his general manager's job, he could be promoted to a Vice Presidency.

I thought, "What have I got to lose?" I flew to Minneapolis for an interview with Gerry and Kamp. I soon had an offer to run the new disk memory business, an operation which had been started a few years before by Tom Kamp.

My starting salary was $32,000 per year, with an option for 1500 shares of CDC common stock at $116 per share; not bad for 1967!

We moved to Minnesota in March, 1968, and bought a lovely home in Minnetonka. I had a twenty minute commute to the Normandale Division, which was named after the street where it was located in Bloomington.

The business of computers and disk memory devices was completely new to me. I understood every technical detail of aircraft instruments, but electronics, bits, and bytes were like a foreign language I couldn't speak.

Tom Kamp remembered me as the technologist who helped him solve some real production problems at Lear, so it was natural for him to assume that I could easily understand computers.

The company had decided to announce the arrival of its 7600 model computer early in 1968. Tom called to tell me that the public announcement, which would be attended by industry experts, customers, and press, was to be made in a few days.

I was to be one of two CDC officials to make the technical presentation. The other person was *Seymour Cray*! The reason that I was picked was that the new disk drive for the 7600 was one of the important performance features of the system.

I tried to explain to Tom that I wasn't knowledgeable enough to make such a presentation, but to no avail. I told Jeanette to go to the library and get anything she could find about computers.

One book she found was a kind of a primer, entitled: "What Is a Computer?" It had all kinds of buzzwords, such as megabytes, transfer rates, bit densities, access times, and byte size.

I wrote a speech geared towards laymen using the book's definitions of these terms, and it went over great. I wasn't asked a single question. I guess everyone thought I was at the Cray level of computer knowledge. Surely, they thought, CDC wouldn't put anyone less knowledgeable than Seymour on the agenda!

The next two years at CDC proved to be highly successful and frustrating. They were successful in the sense that the disk business became very profitable and was growing at a furious rate.

The original equipment manufacturing (OEM) business, where we sold disk drives to systems manufacturers such as

Honeywell, Siemens, and ICL, grew from about $20 million per year to over $200 million by 1970, and on to over $1 billion by the mid-1970s. We sold to every big computer maker in the world, except IBM.

Managing that business profitably, without losing control at those growth rates, was perhaps my greatest management accomplishment.

Despite this success, I once came close to quitting CDC.

G.G. Smith, who was nicknamed "Go-Go," was very difficult to work with. As is sometimes the case with extremely intelligent people, Gerry had no patience with those who were less intelligent. This applied to most of his colleagues, and, unfortunately, he treated us accordingly.

Gerry was extremely aggressive and demanding, and often interfered with the management of the business. He had supreme confidence in himself and outwardly displayed little confidence in anyone else.

One result was that he repeatedly would give orders to my subordinates without my knowledge. I handled this by telling my staff to accept all directives from Gerry, but to make sure they informed me of each order.

After what I felt was one episode too many, I thought seriously about leaving CDC. I did not leave, however, because I felt my short tenure at CDC, which was about one year at that time, would be a serious detriment to obtaining a reasonable management-level job in another company.

Two years at Lear Jet and only one at CDC would look a little like "job-hopping."

A bigger problem for the company was the classic one of failing to keep in step with the quickly advancing technology in disk memory products. The situation began when the innovative engineers, who essentially kept the company alive, headed by Lloyd Thorndyke, had revolted against Gerry Smith because of his attitude.

Lloyd is, in my opinion, the best "hands-on", innovative, and competent engineer I have ever known. He is also the best technical team leader I've known.

Lloyd and his entire crew, consisting of several engineers, had refused to work for Gerry. Before I had started to work for CDC, they had been moved out of the division to a newly created "Research" unit by Bill Norris, CDC's president, simply to hold the design team together.

Norris knew that losing Lloyd completely would be a serious problem for CDC. After I arrived and took Gerry's job, Lloyd and crew still would not come back to the disk business, because Gerry was still in the chain of command.

There are many "tough" corporate managers who wouldn't put up with such insubordination, and would take action by firing these engineers. That might be acceptable if the company had a great depth of talent, but CDC did not have anyone even close to Lloyd, and it showed.

Gerry was an excellent production engineer, and he concentrated on maximizing production efficiency and profits. He had the engineering department spending most of its time supporting products which had been pushed much too quickly into production.

As a result, nothing new was being developed in the disk drive business. In fact, there was not enough engineering talent to solve some critical design problems that were showing up as failures in the field.

The company was starting to have financial problems, as entire mainframe systems failed to perform after installation. Moreover, there were delivery problems with the 6600 model supercomputer system.

Each of these problems affected several million dollars of revenue.

Our most serious problem was with the new 6600 disk file. As I recall, it stored only 130 megabytes of data, but it was six feet tall, three feet wide and ten feet long, weighing over a thousand pounds. It sold for $300,000 at the OEM price and it didn't work very well.

It had oil leaks from the huge hydraulic actuators. The 26-inch diameter discs were subject to contamination from oil and dust. This made the error rate excessively high. We had "head crashes," where the data reading device, or "head," became obstructed, mutilating the disc and destroying the data.

Customers would get pretty upset.

Prior to my arrival in March, 1968, Lloyd Thorndyke had convinced corporate management to stop shipping these units. He got himself assigned as special task force leader to clean up the mess at Normandale.

Production and delivery of CDC systems were far behind schedule because of the quality problems, and the "stop ship" made the situation more difficult. However, Lloyd was not at all impressed with some aerospace engineer that Tom Kamp and Gerry Smith had brought in to run the disk business. He was going to run a thorough engineering/manufacturing investigation and fix the product, no matter how long it took.

In the meantime, the company's revenue was going to hell.

My problem was how to put up with a belligerent corporate task force and get some sort of production schedule under way.

I made a deal with Lloyd. I told him he could take full responsibility for re-engineering the disk drive, using both his and my engineering people. He was welcome to put changes in place as soon as possible.

Since the biggest problem was the disk's error rate, I decided to understand exactly what that meant to the system. It turned out that while we didn't meet our advertised specifications, there were error correction schemes in the system. These schemes let the disk operate reasonably well, despite the high occurrence of errors.

This reminded me of the vertical gyro at Lear which didn't meet spec, but performed satisfactorily in an airplane. It was my old "Will it fly the plane?" situation.

I proposed to Lloyd that we start a program where each disk drive shipped would be required to exceed the performance of the previous drive, until we reached the specified error rate levels. This goal would be reached when Lloyd had all of his changes incorporated.

Lloyd agreed to this program. After a few months, we had everything back on schedule, with our disks operating to the original specifications. We hadn't shipped anything that wouldn't work satisfactorily in the field.

One of our customers was International Computers, Limited (ICL) in London. Their system didn't have the same error recovery scheme as the CDC 7600, so having error-free disk drives was critical to their business.

The managing director's name at ICL was E.C.H. Organ; we called him "Echo." He and Tom Kamp had become very good friends.

That was one of Tom's great assets: his ability to get close to the highest level executives of our customers. He literally became best of friends with each of them, including

Clancy Spangle at Honeywell, Don Eckdahl at NCR, and Organ at ICL. He was a great example of salesmanship and management, in that Tom gave these people his word that CDC would perform. He meant it, and more importantly, they knew he meant it.

I first met Echo Organ during our trials and tribulations with the big disk drives, which the British dubbed "Big Willies."

I tried my "Will it fly the plane?" story on Echo. He looked at me and said, "I say, it's a damned good thing your disk drives don't fly!"

We eventually got things straightened out with ICL, and Echo and I also became good friends.

In spite of these problems and frustrations, I grew in stature with Tom Kamp and other CDC executives. In 1970, I was made Vice President of the Disk Memory Division. I still reported to Gerry Smith.

About a year later, I had a phone call one morning from Tom's personnel chief. He told me that Gerry was being removed as Group Vice President, and I was to take his place. I would report to Tom, and would be responsible for the Normandale Disk Division, Omaha Division (disk fabrication), Rochester Printer Division, and Valley Forge Tape Division.

The next day, Gerry was put on Bill Norris' staff and I was made the new Group Vice President. I'm sure Gerry thought I was a part of a plot to remove him. In fact, I had never expressed my personal frustration about him to anyone, except my wife.

Gerry actually had done a great deal for CDC. He started very successful computer component plants in Redwood Falls, Minnesota, and Rapid City, South Dakota.

He was primarily responsible for starting CDC's disk drive company in Portugal. Unfortunately, he wasn't given much credit for this.

There was a very formal dedication of the Portuguese facility, with attendance by CDC executives and the president of Portugal, Admiral Tomas. This was 1972, shortly after my promotion to Group Vice President.

Gerry, Bill Keye, who was the CDC vice chairman, and I were invited to the ceremony. Bill and I were given medals by the President of Portugal. Gerry's name wasn't even mentioned. In my opinion, this was a travesty.

Gerry was quite a guy. I recall having been introduced to him in a meeting years before at Lear. There were 30 people in the room to hear a presentation from Gerry, who was brand new to the company. His newness was not going to stop Gerry from telling us what was wrong with Lear, Inc.

But, before he made his presentation, he gave a little demonstration of his memory. He had all of us quickly tell him our names and birthdates. A little later, he went around the room at random and repeated every name and birthdate correctly.

I don't care if there was a trick to this feat, I was impressed!

There are endless stories about Gerry. When he first lived in Grand Rapids, he and his family lived on a lovely lake and had a small ski boat. Gerry would bring a friend home and demonstrate his waterskiing prowess.

He had his wife, Lil, pull him off the dock on waterskis, fully dressed in a suit: trousers, shirt, and tie, minus only his shoes and socks. They would spin around the lake until Lil would buzz close enough to shore so that Gerry could make a landing as dry as can be.

I once had a waterskiing incident with Gerry. It was in Minnesota, during the time I worked for him. I also kept a ski boat on Lake Minnetonka, where his family lived.

We were visiting the Smiths one Sunday afternoon and Jeanette's parents happened to be with us. I had taken my boat over to the Smiths'.

We were all sitting on the beach, when Gerry said to me, "Let's give your folks a thrill. I'll sit here in the lawn chair with the skis on, and with the rope coiled in front of me. You hit full throttle on the boat, and it will pop me right onto the water, and I'll ski around the bay."

I told Gerry my boat was awfully powerful and I didn't think that would work, but he insisted. With my teenaged daughter, Susan, acting as a spotter, we rigged everything up and took off at full speed.

Gerry flew out of the chair about six feet into the air, and then was pulled into the water. He disappeared! But, he didn't let go! My daughter was yelling, "You're drowning Mr. Smith, you're drowning Mr. Smith!"

All you could see was the taut rope vibrating as if it had a big fish on the end. Before I could slow down, Gerry popped out of the water and yelled at me to keep going. He got his balance and stayed up for a nice spin around the bay.

Gerry must have hurt all over, but he gave no sign of it. He sure gave the folks a thrill!

When I took over as Group Vice President, Gerry was no longer in the chain of command. That was my opportunity to get Lloyd Thorndyke back into the disk development business.

I knew Lloyd wouldn't go back if only Tom Kamp and I asked him, so I went to Bill Norris and suggested that he ask Lloyd to come back into the mainstream business. Norris did exactly that, and Lloyd came back to do what he did best: develop new and innovative memory products.

The products Lloyd's crew developed between 1971 and 1973 carried CDC's peripheral products business for ten years. This is an excellent example of how continuing development in leading technology pays off in business.

If you are in a high-tech business, you had better be sure you are ready for the "next" product. If you don't spend enough research and development money to bring out competitive, if not leading, products for every new product generation, you might as well fold up your tent or sell out fast.

In 1968, CDC had sued IBM for unfair marketing practices. IBM wanted to stop customers' orders for CDC's 6600 and 7600 computers with promises of forthcoming products.

While the lawsuit was in progress, Tom Kamp decided that CDC should go into the IBM "plug compatible" disk drive business. IBM's very high retail price gave a likely high profit opportunity, if one could go directly to the end user and undersell IBM with a unit that would simply plug into the IBM connector.

I was very much against this approach, because I felt this would put us at the mercy of IBM, who could lower prices at any time, or mess us up with some software change. This approach would also present a problem with CDC's systems business, because we were charging equally high retail prices for our drives when they were sold with one of our systems.

Our prices for our OEM drives were low enough not to be affected if IBM lowered their retail prices. OEM products, which were sold to big computer companies who did not build their own disk drives, were in effect sold at wholesale prices. Costs for us to manufacture these units were relatively quite low, because of the large volumes involved.

We made good profits at the lower prices for OEM drives. However, we made *huge* profits on the same drives when they were sold at retail prices as part of CDC systems.

Tom addressed my objections using a typical Kamp approach. He formed a new division to run the "end user" disk business, which reported to him and bypassed me. It included a full management team: President, Vice President, product management, marketing, accounting, system design, and a maintenance support group.

To me, adding all of this overhead to what I thought was a risky business in the first place would eventually spell trouble.

IBM, in all its arrogance, could not believe that CDC could design equivalent products without copying proprietary IBM designs. They watched us like a hawk. Other people in the industry were doing exactly what IBM suspected, but we weren't. We were doing our own original work, and in fact had better designers than IBM.

Shortly after we had entered the IBM plug compatible business, IBM came out with a new system, called the Model 3330. It was a very advanced unit, with high bit and track densities.

If one were in the IBM plug compatible business, then one had to keep up, which was another problem. It meant that CDC had to design an equivalent of the 3330, whether we wanted to or not.

Of course, our OEM customers needed this competitive product, so there was reason to work on the design. We had already started engineering a new generation of disk drives.

However, now the problem was that IBM had made a drive and controller so interdependent that one couldn't simply plug in a drive alone. A separate controller had to be provided as part of a disk memory system.

To remain in the end user plug compatible business required the design of a very complex controller. We didn't need to do this for OEM customers, for they would contribute their own, as always.

This marked the beginning of a very costly venture which eventually was dropped by CDC. In my opinion, the diversion of funds and effort from the always-profitable OEM business, and the tens of millions of dollars in expenses spent on the end user disk business, contributed to CDC losing the $1.5 billion OEM disk memory business.

While we were designing our version of the 3330 disk drive, the Telex Corporation came to us with an OEM order. We negotiated our largest-ever OEM production contract for 3330 drives for $90 million.

Telex were already in the IBM plug compatible business in other products, and had hired two fairly high-level IBM disk memory and controller engineers to design the controller.

It was not unusual to receive production orders for products not yet designed. It was a gutsy way to do business, but I usually couldn't otherwise get CDC funding for product design.

As a result, we would go after production contracts, then defer the engineering costs until we completed the design. Once we started shipping, we would pay the deferred costs. We had so much profit margin in our OEM business (over 50 percent) that I didn't have to be too accurate in pricing to have enough to pay the deferred costs and still make very significant profits.

At the time we received the Telex contract, we were making so much money that I could self-fund the engineering costs. I decided not to defer the Telex costs, partly because we didn't need to take that approach, and partly because I didn't trust Telex and the end user plug compatible business.

This was the smartest thing I ever did, because as it turned out, we never got to full production with the Telex unit.

We were behind schedule in our design of the 3330 unit and it was becoming a problem with Telex. The top management at Telex kept pushing and asked if we needed help with the design.

It was clear to me that they wanted their "IBM people" to give us IBM secrets. They had misjudged their ex-IBM engineers and CDC, because I refused to have any part of using IBM proprietary data. The two IBM guys were vehement in their refusal to have any part in such a maneuver as well.

We informed Telex of what our delayed schedule was and proceeded with our own design.

While this design process was going on, I received a package that my secretary said had suddenly appeared on her desk. It had my name on it, but she didn't know who delivered it. I opened it and found a rather comprehensive set of drawings of the IBM 3330 unit.

I picked up the phone and called our lawyers at the Oppenheimer law firm. They were handling the IBM lawsuit. Bob Hawkins, of Oppenheimer, asked if I had made copies of the drawings. I had not done so, and knew better than to do that, so he said, "Don't let that data get out of your hands. Just sit there until our courier gets there and give it to him."

We did that and our law firm immediately notified the IBM lawyers. I think IBM always believed that we had copied this information, but we didn't.

The Oppenheimer lawyers later told me they thought we might have lost the lawsuit if I had kept or copied the drawings. Certainly we would not have been given the very favorable settlement we later made with IBM.

We completed the design and started shipping our version of the 3330 to Telex and others. Telex, however, was very far behind in their schedule, partly because of us but also because they were late with their controller design. It seems their two ex-IBM guys wouldn't use their IBM data in the controller design, either.

I always have admired both of these fellows because they had given up great careers at IBM on the basis of promises of glory and riches from Telex.

Telex was in so much trouble that they couldn't pay their bills. Gordon Brown, who headed OEM Sales, and I were pretty much the joint program managers of this huge $90 million contract. We would travel often to Tulsa to stay on top of the Telex situation.

Gordon is one of the world's great salesmen. He was so sincere and likeable that it was easy and fun for me to meet customers with him. They loved him and he always came through for them.

We made a great team and traveled together often. He was always telling stories which were fairly clean when compared to Bill Lear's stories.

One of Gordon's favorites was about the two brothers on the farm who had twin prize pigs. One of the brothers was gone for a few days, during which time one of the pigs died. When he returned home, the other brother said, "Gee, your pig died."

Each of our trips to Telex appeared to be the last. Gordon and I were sure each time that Telex would cancel our contract.

Once, Telex had scheduled a meeting at a time when Gordon was committed to a visit to Japan. Telex wouldn't change the date, so I told Gordon to go on to Japan and that I was sure I could handle whatever came up at Telex. Gordon went to Japan and I went to Tulsa, where Telex informed me that the contract was being canceled.

When I got back to Minneapolis, I sent Gordon a telegram in Japan, which simply said, "Dear Gordon: Your pig died." The Japanese received the message, and interrupted a very high-level meeting to inform Gordon of the very sad news that his pig had died.

The Japanese were a little confused but very sorry to hear of this tragedy. I think they would have been even more sorry if they had realized we had just lost the biggest contract in CDC history!

Telex wasn't the only order that we had lost over the years. Sometimes our competition was our customer. Honeywell, for example, almost always would try to design the next generation disk drive and tell us they would not be buying our product the next time around.

One time, shortly after this had happened, I was addressing a group of security analysts. One of them asked me about not having Honeywell's order. I explained that we wouldn't miss it because of our increasing new orders from other customers. Besides, Honeywell would be back.

In response to why I thought that, I said something to the effect that Honeywell didn't have enough experience to design state-of-the-art disk memories. I felt that they would fail in their attempt and come to us to bail them out.

It was a pretty arrogant and dumb thing to say, for I let myself get set up. An analyst recorded my comments and sent the tape to Jim Binger, the Chairman of Honeywell.

Tom Kamp called me into his office shortly afterwards and said that someone at CDC had "slandered" Honeywell in a talk; Binger wanted that person fired. Tom said Binger was going to call Bill Norris, and that one of us needed to inform Norris ahead of time. Since Tom was going out of town, I should do it. Tom thought this was appropriate, especially after I told him it was probably I who did the slandering.

When I went into Norris's office, he said, "I hear you've done something wrong."

I told him what had happened and he said "Ah, is that all? That's no problem, you told the truth, didn't you?"

I said yes, but the problem is that Binger is going to call him.

Norris stated that Jim Binger wouldn't do that.

I said, "But if he does, what are you going to say?"

Norris got irritated, looked at me and said, "I'll say, 'Piss on you, Binger!'"

That was the end of the conversation and the incident. Guess what? Honeywell came back to us that year and bought more drives than any other customer. They never did design a good disk drive.

When the IBM lawsuit was in its fourth year of discovery and the trial was underway, it looked like CDC was going to win. IBM approached CDC and suggested that a group of CDC executives be on a "settlement team."

One part of the settlement was to be a $25 million contract given to CDC by IBM. CDC was to develop technology for IBM that was yet to be defined. I was on a team of CDC people who visited IBM executives to exchange thoughts on development. We openly discussed projects we had underway.

In one meeting, I described a program which Tom Kamp had authorized after an ex-IBM program manager, who was then at CDC, convinced Tom that the project would be similar to IBM's next generation memory device. It was called a "tape library" and consisted of many small tape cartridges stored in a "beehive" container. Cartridges were accessed by a "picker" and placed in a read/write station.

It was a mechanical and software nightmare, but Tom was sure we could develop the product and be in the end user market at the same time as IBM. We were spending millions of dollars on this monstrosity.

When I described this project to the IBM team, one of the senior executives took me aside and said, "A lot of people follow IBM, but you should know we don't do everything right. You folks shouldn't be spending much on that project, we have abandoned it."

I reported this conversation to Tom and Norris, but we went right on and didn't stop until the project had cost us millions.

As part of the ongoing legal process, the IBM lawyers were taking depositions from senior CDC executives. My turn came at a time when I had decided to quit smoking. My deposition lasted eight full days. The IBM lawyers were determined to dig up some kind of dirt in the disk drive or end user business.

On each morning of the deposition, we went through a little ritual. The senior IBM lawyer was a heavy smoker. He would sit down across from me each morning and lay out an array of smoking material: pipe, pipe tobacco, filter cigarettes, regular cigarettes, and small cigars.

I would lay out several packages of mints, such as Lifesavers and breath mints. The lawyer would puff away, sending smoke in my direction. I would crunch on the candy mints.

I knew that if I ever got through this, I would never smoke again. I haven't.

Both IBM and CDC legal staffs were loaded with material collected over a four-year discovery period. CDC built a database system for the suit and computerized its information. This allowed counsel to respond instantly on any issue. The IBM lawyers plugged away, using paper and pen only.

The IBM attorney at my deposition had volumes of memos from inside CDC with which he used to "confront" me.

One memo in particular was embarrassing. It was a memo from Gordon Brown, the salesman, to Tom Kamp expressing Gordon's concern about my organization being behind schedule with our version of 3330 for Telex. Gordon had ended his memo with the comment, "John must improve this schedule if he has to beg, borrow, or steal!"

The IBM lawyer had me read the memo and then said, "Mr. Titsworth, *did you* beg, borrow or steal?"

One could see why IBM thought we stole their design!

By 1972, I had been promoted to Executive Vice President of Peripheral Products, and Tom was President. I had responsibility for all operations except the end user division, which Tom kept under his supervision, along with the marketing and legal departments.

Our part of the company brought in nearly $1 billion in annual revenue, and it was making most of CDC's profits during 1972 to 1974.

Computer Services was an emerging business and was getting much corporate support from Norris and Bob Price, who at that time was President of Systems and Services.

Commercial Credit was generating over $1 billion of revenue per year, and had made money since its acquisition in 1968.

In 1974, CDC lost $80 million in the computer systems business. That business was a shambles and out of control.

To my great surprise, Bob Price called one day and offered me the presidency of the computer business, including the main Systems Division, the Military Aerospace Division, and the emerging Energy Management business. I was also to run the Canadian operations, which included sales, the systems manufacturing and engineering business, and an aerospace company we owned in Canada.

It was a big promotion, with the corporate title of "Executive Vice President, Systems."

It was also the world's biggest challenge. Besides being embroiled in a number of multi-million dollar contracts that had been underestimated technically and financially, Bill Norris had announced publicly after our disaster year that, "nobody can make money in the computer systems business. We at Control Data are going to make our future in computer services!"

CDC had acquired its Service Bureau from IBM as part of the settlement of the lawsuit. After one of our "Settlement Team" visits to IBM, where we reviewed their organization in detail, I suggested to Norris that CDC should get the Service Bureau as part of the settlement.

Bill Norris was convinced that the future was in services. He was very pragmatic and honestly believed we could not make money in *systems*. Norris looked at the positive side of his argument, which was that CDC could be a great *services* company.

His public statements convinced Wall Street, our bankers, and all of our customers that we were going out of the systems business. I not only had to get us out of impossible contracts and modernize our product line, but I had to find a way to keep old customers and get new ones, most of whom thought we wouldn't be around.

As I have mentioned previously, I was not a computer expert. However, I was knowledgeable enough to know what one could and couldn't do with a computer. It was obvious to me that it took more than super-fast hardware to solve an applications problem.

It seemed to me that if you were going to supply the banking industry with big computers, you needed to know something about banks and bank transactions. Unfortunately, we had entered the banking industry and we knew as much about banking as the bankers knew about computers, which wasn't very much at all.

We had also agreed to automate the entire Air Force Logistics system with our mainframes. This and the bank project were two of many contracts that I felt were not in our field of expertise.

My assessment of the CDC Systems problem was that we had strayed from our strength, which was *scientific* computing. We knew how to do seismic data processing for the oil industry; we knew how to simulate wind tunnels; we knew how to process weather data; we knew how to perform computer-aided design; we knew how to do image processing; we knew how to analyze power distribution and control for electric utilities. Why were we messing around in non-scientific areas?

We were in these commercial areas because our salesmen had been given a free hand to sell to anyone, anywhere in any business. They were doing exactly that, and unfortunately were very successful. The sales force did not report to me, so I had to find a way to curb their ambitions.

It was easy! I wrote a memo to the sales force which said that Systems would not honor any contract involving the delivery of a mainframe, unless my signature was on the contract.

I established strategic business areas, which included: Petroleum, Energy Management, Weather, Computer-Aided Design, and Government Systems. This last category involved weapons research; we could simulate very closely the explosion of an atomic bomb. The salesmen were told that anything outside these strategic areas wouldn't have any hope of reaching my desk.

Task teams were assigned to recover basic costs and extricate us from our most troubled contracts. These customers included the Bank of Switzerland, the Canadian Post Office, and the Air Force Logistic System.

I had a hell of a team of executives! Bob Duncan was the chief engineer of Systems, Bill Fitzgerald was the chief financial officer, Boyd Jones was head of Government Systems, Lloyd Thorndyke was head of Research Labs (and later head of Star (Cyber 100) Super Computers), Mike Kaye headed the Aerospace Division, George Hubbs ran Canada, Shelly Tart ran Energy Management, and Norm Skinner was the head of Computer Manufacturing. There was never a more competent group of people or those better suited to serve in their positions.

I had two great managers: Bob Price, my immediate supervisor, and Bill Norris. They gave me the freedom to do what had to be done, and I got their support when I needed it.

The industry, media, and financial community haven't treated them well, and that's a shame. When I worked for them, they were attentive, well-informed, and decisive executives.

Bill Norris was a visionary leader with a social conscience. This country could use more of those assets. Some of his programs didn't succeed financially, but they were mismanaged by subordinates. I believe this was because he didn't have the "cream of the crop" running those businesses. Those operations were very tough to run. Despite such shortcomings, CDC did experience success in the last half of the 1970s.

Bill Norris was a risk taker in more ways than one. Each year, I would bet him that Systems would improve the bottom line by several millions of dollars. My biggest win was in 1978, when we made $30 million in profit. In four years, we had improved Systems profits by $100 million, and reduced assets from $600 million to $300 million.

Bill paid my bets with 100 crisp one dollar bills in front of the Board of Directors. He also would comment on how he got more out of that $100 than any bonus he ever gave.

Bill actually got more out of that bet than he knew. Each year, I would let each of my officers have part of the bet. They all wanted part of Bill Norris' $100.

With a team as good as I had in Systems, I had an interesting role to play. I couldn't add to the technical prowess or manufacturing expertise, so I became the defender of the underdogs, the keeper of the faith, the Pied Piper of Systems. I made speech after speech about our scientific capability and our responsiveness to customer needs.

I made these speeches to our own people, to customers, to user groups, to sister operations such as Services, and to the sales organizations. I quite often started my talk by making an announcement. I would announce that the audience should not be concerned, because, "CDC is not going out of the *Services* business!" It would always bring the house down.

I would also poke fun at people. I would introduce Bob Duncan, who was a Texan, as our "educated Texan." I would then explain that an educated Texan was someone we had taught to say, "Isn't that incredible!" instead of "No shee-it!"

I would also poke fun at myself by starting my talks, especially to new employee groups, by saying that I understood that John Titsworth was an unusual name, and that some of them were embarrassed with it. Therefore, I wanted them to know that they could call me "Sam" Titsworth.

When I walked through the factory, people would say, "Hey, Sam!" or "Hi, Sam!" and we all would smile. It broke the ice and I think my employees knew I was nothing more than simply one of them.

The twelve years at CDC were the best of my career. I often wonder what would have happened if I had stayed. Could I have helped prevent the disasters that occurred at CDC in the 1980s? I don't know, but it might have been fun to try.

I know this: I would have had more freedom to try, more authority, and far less bureaucracy than I had experienced at Xerox, my subsequent employer.

VI

XEROX: THE CHALLENGE

One evening in the fall of 1978, I was relaxing in my recliner, alternately glancing at television and going through my business mail, which I always brought home from the office.

On the end table next to the telephone was the latest copy of Fortune magazine. The cover had a picture of a fellow dressed like Uncle Sam in his classic World War II pose, saying, "I want you." I had read the cover story, which was about executive recruiting companies. The article featured the firm of Heidrick and Struggles, which was located in New York and Chicago.

The phone rang and a man said: "Mr. Titsworth, you probably don't know who we are, but I'm with Heidrick and Struggles in New York and we would like to talk to you about a job opportunity."

I assured him that I knew who he was, and added that I was not interested in leaving Control Data. He quickly commented that he was quite aware of my success at CDC, and knew that I was in a very good position there. He added that the "opportunity" to which he referred was something I couldn't afford not to hear about in person.

It was a pleasant conversation and I finally agreed to meet him at a local hotel later that week.

At our first meeting, my recruiter was obviously more interested in checking me out than in describing the opportunity. He wouldn't tell me the name of the company, but he described the position as a group vice presidency in a leading East Coast company. This company was run by a fairly young fellow who he described as, "good enough to be about anything he wanted to be, including President of the United States."

I told the recruiter that he didn't have to name the company, it had to be Xerox Corporation. After the two-hour interview, which I thought went very well, he told me that he would be back in touch.

I heard nothing further until November, when another recruiter from the same firm called to say that the first recruiter had been hired by another firm. Their client, however, was very interested in me, but before we went any further, the new recruiter wanted to come out to Minneapolis and meet me.

Heidrick and Struggles nearly lost me with their change in recruiters, because I was not very interested in starting over. However, the new guy seemed to be a very sincere person, so I agreed to meet him. His name was Ray Klemmer, and he turned out to be the best professional recruiter I've known. We became friends and still stay in touch.

A few weeks later, I had an invitation to come to Stamford, Connecticut, for a dinner with David Kearns, the President of Xerox. At that dinner, I found him to be everything that I had heard.

Kearns was an energetic, articulate fellow who appeared to know what he wanted. He wanted an executive whose management style would foster an entrepreneurial, non-bureaucratic, and profit-oriented environment for a number of fairly independent businesses.

These businesses consisted of acquisitions and internal divisions of Xerox, and collectively were called the Information Products Group (IPG). These operations included Shugart Associates, Versatec Corporation, Diablo Systems, Century Data Corporation, Xerox Computer Services, El Segundo Operations, and the Dallas operations. Later, in 1980, Western Union International and Kurzweil Computer Products were added.

The Palo Alto Research Center (PARC) was not included in IPG. However, Kearns was concerned with gaining leverage from the $40 million per year which went into PARC. Essentially, he wanted me to help him take PARC's ideas and potential products to market.

After our meeting in November, I heard nothing for several weeks, so I called Kearns. He said they were having extensive discussions about whether or not to go outside Xerox for such a high position. They had one internal candidate.

There was also trouble with internal members of Xerox's Board of Directors regarding my insistence on becoming a Board member.

After a few more weeks, I got a call asking my wife and me to come to Stamford for another dinner. The dinner would be followed with a series of meetings the next day with the Chairman of the Board, Peter McColough, and several other members of the Board's Management Committee.

The night before I left for Stamford, I told Klemmer that I would not insist on Board membership immediately, but that I expected it after the first year. Kearns' word on that was good enough for me.

I knew I couldn't mess up the operation in one year, and I knew Kearns would keep his word. It only takes one meeting between honest business people to know each other's character. Kearns and I always had a good and trusting relationship. Although my interaction with McColough was limited, I felt the same way about him.

All the interviews seemed to go well. It was interesting to see what each member of the Management Committee had on his mind.

The Chairman primarily was interested in one thing: can I present the proper Xerox image to the business world? He mentioned this several times, and there was no question about how important he thought this was.

Jim O'Neil, an executive vice president, had responsibility for copier manufacturing and engineering. He was the most helpful of all the people with whom I interviewed. I got a straightforward view of the difficulties of running this group of operations.

It seems that everyone at the top level of Xerox management had "broken his pick" on the Information Products Group at one time or another. Jim all but said that I should forget this job and remain in the happy environment of CDC.

Despite this, I started my third career in March, 1979, in Stamford at the Xerox international headquarters on Long Ridge Road.

The building was fairly new but unattractive on the outside, which was grey pre-formed concrete. It looked like a cross between a prison and a fortress. Employees joked that we could simply push the cannon to the front windows when IBM came charging up the hill.

The inside of the building was quite attractive, with spacious lobbies and halls decorated with high quality paintings and sculptures.

However, the offices were of modest size and spartan in decor. They were nothing like what the general public believes corporate offices should be, and did not have the opulence I've seen in corporations like GTE or U.S. Steel.

Despite the exterior, Xerox's corporate headquarters was done well and it was an extremely pleasant work environment.

Jeanette and I looked for a place to live in the Stamford area. We finally settled on a three-acre "estate" in New Canaan.

Our house was in the Southern Colonial style, with six tall classical pillars and a huge porch across the entire front. With 6,000 square feet and only two of us, it seemed a bit excessive, but I must say it was a beautiful and elegant establishment. We even had a fenced paddock for horses.

At times I think some things in life are backwards. What a place this New Canaan home would have been to raise our four children, who were now grown up and on their own. Instead, in our earlier years, we had struggled with barely adequate dwellings. On the other hand, maybe that's how one ends up with a loving and close family.

I must say that my children, John, Steven, Susan, and Sandra, absolutely are the best kids anyone could have. John has become a sales executive in the computer industry. Steven is a highly successful mortgage broker, and Susan is now a dental hygienist, homemaker, and mother. Sandra is a beautiful young lady who excels as a legal secretary.

We soon joined "The" Congregational Church of New Canaan. Jeanette sang in the choir and I soon found myself on the Board of Trustees with responsibilities for facilities and grounds.

Most of my Xerox operations were located in California. Xerox Computer Services, El Segundo Operations (the old SDS Corporation), Century Data Corporation and the work going on for the new network systems were in the Los Angeles area. Versatec, Diablo, Shugart, and PARC were in the San Francisco area. The Office Products Division was located in Dallas, and had responsibility for word processors and fac-simile products.

While Kearns and I were negotiating my terms, I wanted to live in California and occasionally travel to Stamford. I felt I could stay on top of things by being close by my operations, a habit I have developed over the years.

When I ran the CDC disk business, I walked every day through engineering or manufacturing in order to talk with the people there. That way, I could really get a clear sense of what was going on.

My last job at CDC was essentially a group position, since I oversaw remote operations run by senior general managers who reported to me in person.

The Xerox job was clearly going to be different! The closest operation was 2,000 miles away, and most of the others were 3,000 miles distant.

I had told Kearns that I did not believe in organizations that had large staffs. Kearns remarked that there were over 400 people who comprised the corporate staff in Stamford. I found out that there were an equal number located in Roch-ester, which is the site of Xerox's copier division headquar-ters. These 800 people interacted mostly with each other.

I was amazed to realize that there was more management staff in Xerox than most companies have as employees!

Dealing with a management staff of 800 sometimes had its humorous side. I'll never forget the time Joe Capretta, who headed copier manufacturing, played a joke on his boss, Jim O'Neil, who was located at corporate headquarters.

Each month Jim would go to Rochester to have an operations review with Joe. Jim had a list of questions prepared by his staff and Joe had a list of answers prepared by his own. Both staffs would meet each month before the operations meeting, and prepare these questions and answers.

This particular time, Jim asked question #1 and Joe gave him the answer to question #3. This went on for a while, until Jim asked Joe what he was doing.

Joe said that each month Jim would ask his questions, and he answered them from his prepared list of answers. Joe thought that was sort of boring, so he wanted to put some excitement into the meeting to see if Jim could match the questions with his answers.

It's funny but sad when you think of the waste of effort putting these questions and answers together, especially since most of the topics were trivial. Joe suggested that they simply exchange lists each month.

There was no way that I was going to have a huge staff. I wanted a small personnel organization, a financial consolidation group, and one or two advisors, one for long range strategy and one for day to day operations, each fairly high level.

I was President of IPG and Group Vice President of Xerox Corporation. I made each of my staff people IPG Vice Presidents. They were Paul Strassmann, V.P. of Strategic Planning, Walter Kirson, V.P. of Finance, Joe Charlton, V.P. of Personnel, and Tom Winter, V.P. of Operations. Connie

Luppino was my administrative assistant; she knew how to run an executive office better than anyone else that I have known.

I had 15 people in all, and 10 of them were in finance, doing productive work on things such as trend analyses, and division and corporate consolidation. Most of these people had been assigned to IPG under Dave Culbertson, my predecessor; in effect I inherited them.

One of the first things I did was to ask around to find what people generally thought of these individuals. I went to Rochester to see Joe Capretta and the infamous Shelby Carter, who had a reputation as the world's best sales executive.

When I asked Carter about one of my staff, he said: "If you gave him a hammer and nail he'd drive it through his pecker!" I decided not to ask about anyone else. I preferred to form my own opinions.

Generally, my staff was made up of good people.

Joe Charlton was as fine a personnel manager as I've known, and my division people liked him. He was genuinely helpful to the division and subsidiary executives, and that's what a good staff person should be.

Walter Kirson was a jewel. He had worked for Xerox's chief financial officer, Mel Howard, both at Ford Motors and Xerox. At Xerox, Walter had put together the consolidation and corporate financial reports for IPG, and had done so while reporting directly to Mel.

I wanted Walter to continue this function, but transfer to my organization, which he did. Mel was concerned that he would be cut off from important data if he didn't have this function reporting to him. I told him that Walter could report to him as well, and this appeared to work satisfactorily.

Tom Winter was someone I had added to the contingent that Culbertson had left. I wanted someone who could establish good communication with each of the group's organizations. This person had to be familiar with the group's daily operations, and at the same time help these organizations work with the corporate staff. He would be the contact for these operations if they needed services from the corporate staff.

Despite their large numbers, Xerox's corporate staff was made up of very capable individuals. The problem was that there was really not much for them to do. Being conscientious, and wanting to be needed and respectable, caused them to create work for themselves. What was worse was that this gave everyone else more work, also.

In the end, I'm sure I had placed Tom Winter in the wrong job. Tom had been a corporate controller, and certainly had a lot of talent in finance. My managers of the various businesses simply didn't like Tom's approach. Tom became terribly frustrated and eventually left. He was replaced by Walter, who did very well.

Paul Strassmann was one of the most knowledgeable computer analysts in the country. His understanding of practical applications and the "do's" and "don'ts" of computers was legendary. When anyone in Xerox had a question about computer applications or statistics, Paul would be called.

If Paul had a problem, it was in answering a question in too abundant detail. Paul has a story about a high-level meeting where some specific computer question arose. When no one knew the answer, it was suggested to David Kearns that someone should find Paul, who would surely know the answer.

David was reported to have said, "Forget it, we don't have that much time."

Paul also knew the printing business. With his computer systems knowhow and intimate familiarity with the printing industry, he was a natural to be chief strategist for IPG, and he did a good job.

After David Kearns insisted that I have my base of operations in Stamford, we agreed that since most of my operating units were on the West Coast, I should maintain a West Coast residence for the extended visits I assumed would take place.

Jeanette and I rented a very nice condo in Palos Verdes, in the hills south of Los Angeles.

I set up an office in the El Segundo facilities, where the new laser printer program and other development of laser applications took place. There was also some work on the Star personal computer and Ethernet network project at El Segundo.

The Dallas operations had just been put under El Segundo. These operations included a word processor product and a low-cost typewriter program called Centaur , along with a declining effort in facsimile. The Dallas and El Segundo operations were organizationally combined under the name Xerox Business Systems (XBS).

Century Data and Xerox Computer Services were also in the Los Angeles area, Century in Anaheim and Xerox Computer Services in Santa Monica. That still left Dallas 2,000 miles away, and Shugart, Versatec, and Diablo in San Francisco, which was over 350 miles away.

My first visit to the West Coast took place in May, 1979, when I tried to become familiar with my people and products, and to get my personal living quarters arrangements made.

The subsidiary operations, Shugart, Versatec, and Diablo, had classic pyramid organizational structures and ran more or less independently.

Shugart, which made floppy disk drives, was on a roll with revenue growth of almost 100 percent per year. It was making very good profits from its OEM business.

Versatec was the only company in the U.S. making electrostatic printers. Its competition came from pen plotters, an older and slower technology. It also was growing at a tremendous rate, and making reasonable profits.

Diablo, which made daisy wheel printers, became less independent when Xerox took more control by appointing a Rochester copier engineer as the general manager. Xerox also allowed the Amalgamated Clothing and Textile Workers union to organize there. This was the same union that represented workers in the copier business.

Diablo led the market, but was an extremely inefficient organization; it lost millions of dollars each year. This was partly because the management didn't understand the OEM business. In addition, Xerox's corporate staff had infiltrated Diablo so that almost all decisions came back to Xerox headquarters for review and extended analysis.

In short, Diablo was a disaster. So was XBS, for many of the same reasons. Absolutely nothing happened without a corporate review.

Xerox's corporate staff was actually a copier business staff. The copier business was organized as one huge function. Both the V.P. of manufacturing and engineering and the V.P. of marketing and sales were in Stamford. The chief financial officer of Xerox was primarily the head of finance for copiers, and he was in Stamford.

The way these people wanted my business to be organized was to have engineering, manufacturing, finance, and sales in each of my operations to report to the head of each of these functions in Xerox corporate. I could not imagine having the chief engineer in Dallas report to someone in Stamford (or Rochester) and the head of manufacturing reporting to someone else in Stamford (or Rochester), with nothing actually coming together until it got to Kearns or me.

In the early 1970s, Xerox had actually tried to operate Xerox Data Systems (XDS), which was the original Scientific Data Systems (SDS) acquisition, with that structure. XDS as a subsidiary corporation was closed down by Xerox in 1974.

Century Data had been purchased during the time I was being recruited. If someone at Xerox had asked me then about the purchase, I would have strongly advised against buying Century. Anyone in the hard disk business in 1979 knew that Century was "out of it." Their products were obsolete, and they had spent nothing on research and development for years.

In view of the fact that we owned Shugart, which was going into the newer generation of 8-inch and 5-inch hard disks, Century certainly was not an asset. If I had made any mistakes with Shugart, it was in suppressing their efforts in the hard disk area in order to give some kind of future to Century.

In other words, I made Shugart stick to floppies and Century stay in hard disk technology. Had we not owned Century, I would have supported Shugart's new generation hard disk efforts, at which I think they could have been very successful. This assumes that we would have been allowed to go offshore for cheap labor and materials.

It was around the first of June, after three months with the company, when I discovered the kind of relationship Xerox had with the Amalgamated Clothing and Textile Workers union.

I was on a one-week golf vacation in a remote area of northern Michigan, an annual event with all my old Lear buddies and our families. This was an event I hadn't missed for twenty years.

I was on the first tee when I was paged by the pro shop. It was Doug Reid, the Vice President of Personnel, who explained that the company wanted me to fire the President of Century Data for publishing an anti-union document.

Apparently the union had asked Xerox if they could make a membership drive at Century, as they had done some years before at Diablo. As I understand it, they had been told that Corporate didn't particularly want a union at Century, but that it would be up to the employees. The union could have an election, Century would not interfere, and everything would be handled in a gentlemanly manner.

Jim Payton, the President and general manager of Century Data, was an aggressive, outgoing and confident leader who, as near as I could tell, was very well liked by his employees. There was no way that any good, red-blooded, profit-oriented, entrepreneurial Californian would allow a union shop to start on his watch.

I don't know if Jim ever knew of Corporate's discussions with the union. I didn't.

When the union showed up, Jim hired a sharp lawyer who wrote up all the legal things management can say to its employees against a union organizing attempt. This document was given to all Century employees. Essentially, it said in effect: "The union cannot guarantee you a raise in pay," "The Company does not want a union," and "It's the opinion of management that the employees will not benefit from a union."

The union went back to Xerox headquarters and reported that the management at Century was clearly anti-union and was not gentlemanly.

That did it! I was ordered to fire the President, and Century was ordered to invite the union in for an election, with not one statement to the employees from management, except, "it's up to you, folks."

I went back to Stamford the next day and had a long meeting with Xerox's Chairman of the Board. It was clear to me that this was a matter of principle with him. Something had to happen.

I'm sure that corporate staff had been told to inform Century Data of the discussion with the union, but that information certainly had not been conveyed clearly or properly.

I have nothing against the union, and God knows too many companies take advantage of employees. However, I always have felt that my relationship with my employees was open, honest, and fair. I simply didn't need the bureaucracy of a union.

I dismissed the President of Century Data, but I made sure that he got a good severance package. In the mean time, the union won the election.

The union had a great deal of leverage at Xerox. This was not because of its relationship with management, but because copiers are a very labor-intensive product; the union knew very well where all the money was being made.

This situation was very significant because any substantial glitch in copier manufacturing would put Xerox in big trouble. The "relationship" between the union and Xerox management was good from necessity, not love.

If you have a union, it's best to do what you can to make living together easy. Things will go much better on friendly, honorable terms than with a belligerent approach.

One of the nicest things said about my beliefs on this subject was by my Vice President of Finance at CDC, Bill Fitzgerald. Nobody is any tougher or better at his job than Bill Fitzgerald. He said he learned from Johnny T. that you can manage better with kindness, compassion, understanding, and genuine concern than by threats and coercion. At least you have the loyalty of the good people.

I have to say that the union had little visible effect on Century Data. That company was too far into a decline in an industry that was crowded with competitors.

I would describe the disk drive business as a capital-intensive, high technology, short product cycle, low margin, commodity business. Even a new MBA could tell that such a business would have little chance of success, even if there were no union.

The union had its eye on Shugart as well, but the situation at that company was far different than the one at Century Data. In contrast, Shugart was making high margins on revenues that grew 100 percent per year.

The management at Shugart included Don Massaro, Jim Bochnowski (a venture capitalist), and Joe Booker. Don and Joe had been founders of Shugart with Al Shugart. Both men were entrepreneurial, charismatic, and aggressive leaders.

Don had made several million dollars at age 34 when Xerox bought Shugart in 1978. Before this occurred, he had been made President when the venture capital company, as the majority owner, demanded that management be replaced when a serious business glitch arose. This may have been one of those rare occasions when the venture capital backers made the right decision.

In any case, Xerox management didn't want to disturb a profit-making operation that Don was running very well.

I knew that Don and the entire management team would walk out if the union were allowed to approach Shugart. There was no doubt that a union environment would not have worked at Shugart. It would have killed the business.

Later, in 1984, by resisting offshore production by Xerox Corporation, the union may have contributed to the demise of this $300 million company; it could have been as successful as Seagate, which became a $2 billion company.

Neither McColough or Kearns wanted to do anything that would upset Don Massaro. They saw in him an entrepreneurial spirit and a gung-ho management style which somehow they wanted to get into the copier side of the company.

How docs one describe Don Massaro? Tall, good looking, confident, articulate, charismatic, fearless, humorous, and aggressive. He was a combination of George Custer, George Patton, and Tyrone Power. You could like him or hate him.

I liked him, Kearns liked him and McColough liked him, but every other *Xerox* person in Corporate and the copier organization hated him with a passion. Don eventually failed at Xerox, which just goes to show that you need support from more than the *Chairman, President,* and *Executive Vice President* in a large corporation.

Such support is purely political, and keeps enemies at bay as long as you are a winner. When you falter, your enemies come down even harder, and your political support fades awfully fast. Whoever heard of the Chairman or President of a company supporting a loser?

But I never gave up on Don. I supported and protected him from corporate staff, the copier people, and my peers. There were times when he didn't deserve support. There were times when he should have been fired.

I had some other colorful people reporting to me.

Renn Zaphiropoulos, the president and founder of Versatec, is probably the most outstanding corporate manager of people in the U.S. He's a showman, an intellectual, a brilliant engineer, an outstanding speaker and teacher, a talented entertainer of professional caliber, an expert in wines, a gourmet cook, an artist, a first-class cabinet maker, and more.

The esprit de corps and loyalty of Versatec employees was something to see. Everyone who worked hard at Versatec was well rewarded financially, and given recognition and praise.

Renn always had profit-related bonuses and profit-sharing programs that were easy to understand, but which required top performance to achieve. When they were earned, they were presented with flair.

During one year, the non-management employees would earn a bonus of 7 percent of salary if the company achieved maximum profitability. Renn kept them in suspense all year.

On the day the results were to be announced, Renn rented a large auditorium and gave a party for all Versatec employees. He kept them waiting and wondering while they were enjoying large quantities of beer and food.

Suddenly, the big doors at one end of the room opened, and in came the Stanford University Band in full regalia, playing a John Philip Sousa march. They were followed by Renn Zaphiropoulos riding the back of a huge elephant that was draped with a banner decorated with a big "7%" in red letters. Renn, with his white hair and distinctive goatee, looked like Buffalo Bill Cody; not a bad comparison in the showmanship category.

Imagine this highly successful leader being told that he couldn't make a news release without Xerox corporate approval, or being lectured by a junior staff specialist on how to set up incentives for his employees! It was downright patronizing, but there was a never-ending stream of directives and corporate advisors going into Versatec, as well as the other units in my group.

This prompted me to prepare a letter defining the working relationship between the IPG group and corporate staff. This was a guideline on how I wanted things to work, and was addressed to my group's division managers and presidents of subsidiaries. The following presents the gist of this memo:

> As you know, I vigorously support decentralization and profit center management for a number of reasons. I believe that when a corporation starts to develop a diverse line of products it must recognize the uniqueness of technologies, markets, and business environment associated with different product lines and tailor the management approach accordingly. Profit center management permits team effort, common goals, and business focus so necessary to success.
>
> We need to find a way to retain the entrepreneurial efforts and 'independence' of IPG units while fulfilling our obligations and responsibility to the parent company. After all, we are *owned* by Xerox and Xerox has a responsibility to its shareholders, not only to report on our performance but also to assure these shareholders that our efforts are in the overall best interest of the corporation.
>
> Now, as to how to work with Headquarters on a day-to-day basis, it has been my intent to establish focal points at Stamford through the establishment of two offices—Vice President-Planning and Vice President-Operations. I don't want a large staff and the only way to avoid it is for Tom Winter and Paul Strassmann to use existing corporate staff personnel to assist them and you. It's clear that the only way to accomplish this efficiently is to have (the corporate staff)

'effectively' report to Tom and Paul. The staff resources must provide a *complimentary service* to your own operation. They should not be a check and balance, policing or monitoring activity, but should render help and support when it's needed.

After the letter was published, the reactions were incredible. A corporate financial officer was reported to have said something like, "This is a disaster!"

Corporate staff people in sales, manufacturing, and strategy were highly indignant, and predicted that nothing would succeed without their continued involvement. The legions of corporate staff never understood that they should be a *service* to the IPG operations, not a *police force*.

I wanted each of my operations to be an autonomous profit center. Of course, I expected them to comply fully with corporate requirements, such as financial reporting and forecasting.

The IPG member companies were expected to present their long range plans and strategies to Corporate on a regular basis. However, I did not require them to comply with every detail, process, or procedure in the copier organization's engineering, personnel, and manufacturing departments. I expected them to use acceptable practices, but they were free to use whatever process they felt best suited their businesses.

As their boss, I expected to be kept fully informed of everything good or bad occurring in their organizations. There was a fairly long list of questions that I wanted answered each month. I got answers through operations reports, and every quarter we would have a face-to-face operations review.

The most important message of my "relationship" memo was that my operations were responsible to me and no one else, certainly not every Tom, Dick and Harry in the Xerox Corporation.

It seemed obvious to me that my primary focus needed to be on the XBS operation. XBS products included the new laser printer in El Segundo, word processors and facsimile products in Dallas, and the PARC-developed Star/Ethernet project in El Segundo and Palo Alto.

The laser printer product was important enough, and potentially a large enough, revenue producer to warrant being an independent operation. As a result, some reorganization was necessary.

The laser printer project became a division and independent profit center with all the elements of a subsidiary, including its own sales and marketing departments. I picked Bob Adams, who ran sales for XBS, to head the newly-formed Printer Systems Division.

The copier organization in Rochester had been campaigning to have the laser printer product transferred to them. It looked an awful lot like a high-speed copier to them.

I agreed to transfer the printer division, but not for Rochester's reasons. I knew it would cost tens of millions of dollars per year to complete the development and market introduction of the new model 9200 printer. I didn't want that loss showing on IPG financial reports, especially on top of other losses we were incurring from startup efforts on new products and the poor performance of older product lines.

It is hard to explain losses in the hundreds of millions of dollars, even when it is budgeted. In good times, you can get away with such "investments," but when times get tough, you don't cut back on the winners. You stop spending money on the losers!

In July, 1979, my organization looked like this from a management perspective:

The Dallas shop was almost an embarrassment to Xerox, due to its poor performance.

 Star/Ethernet was still in an early development stage.

Diablo and Century Data needed new leadership.

All that Versatec, Shugart, and Xerox Computer Services needed was to be left alone and protected from corporate staff.

As is true with most corporations in trouble, the solution was related to organizational structure, lines of communication, and, most importantly, leadership. The most prominent example of finding solutions through leadership is the success of Chrysler Corporation with Lee Iacocca.

While cash was not considered a problem in my group, I felt certain operations were worth spending cash on, and others were not.

I had been asked by one of my colleagues at Corporate if I thought I could get my part of the company on a respectable performance level and Xerox well established as an office automation company.

I said yes, but it would be a race to see if I could get there before the company ran out of cash.

He laughed and asked if I knew that Xerox had $1 billion in cash.

I said I knew that, but because of the way Xerox spent cash, that money wouldn't last long.

It's ironic that in 1984, four years later, the company had to consider selling and leasing back its headquarters building because they were low on cash. I know for sure that I did not spend *all* of it by myself.

Nevertheless, cash considerations entered my decision process in choosing new leaders for Diablo and Century Data.

The general manager of Diablo was trying to run that company like Xerox in Rochester, New York, with all of its staff-oriented bureaucracy. Diablo needed to be a much more responsive OEM-oriented business, and needed a leader who understood the OEM business.

Dallas didn't have a leader. That organization was structured so that the engineering department in Dallas reported to someone in El Segundo, as did the rest of the departments. Dallas needed an on-site, full-time leader.

The Century Data general manager had been fired because of the union fiasco. I wanted someone at Century Data who could keep absolute control, contain the losses, and rebuild the business *slowly* with minimum negative cash flow. This would take a dedicated, quiet, work-around-the-clock, solid (but not a showman), and likeable bottom-line-oriented executive.

I found him in El Segundo, where he ran engineering and manufacturing. Jim Conway was just the ticket for Century Data. In three years he rebuilt Century's reputation, and with upgrades in old product lines, actually established a reasonable OEM business.

Jim was such a dedicated and honest executive that customers trusted him to do a good job, and he did. I think he could have turned Century Data into a good little company, but after I left in 1983, corporate staff got back in the way.

After I left, when OEM customers asked the usual question when placing new large orders: "Do you expect to be in business for the next year?", legal staff refused to let anyone say "yes." New orders dried up, and that was the end of Century.

Xerox sold Century Data in the late 1980s on an earn-out basis (no cash), and wrote the new owner a check for several million dollars to cover pension and other benefit liabilities to employees.

Xerox headquarters was continually submitting people to me for consideration to fill jobs in IPG. They were all copier people from sales or expatriates from Rank Xerox, the British affiliate. They all were in between jobs, which meant no one knew what to do with them.

Xerox was no different than most international corporations who find it very difficult to reinstate or integrate back into the system those people who complete a tour of duty overseas.

Each and every candidate thought he was capable and ready to run one of the "little" two or three hundred million dollars per year IPG businesses. None of them had ever worked in an area other than sales, or whatever discipline to which they had been assigned since starting with Xerox.

The copier business was so massive that such employees never gained experience outside their own area. Most of them had been promoted and given a raise every 12 to 18 months like clockwork for 10 or 15 years, so they made $70 to $80 thousand per year, plus a bonus.

At that level, the only job I could have given them would be a general manager's position. I had only one or two of those open, and Diablo's top position was one.

Imagine hiring someone whose only claim to fame was consistent promotions and pay raises in accounting (or sales, or manufacturing) departments to be the President and general manager of a $200 million corporation! This showed that these acquired subsidiaries were given no stature or recognition, nor were they considered a significant part of Xerox Corporation by the copier organization.

There was one person who struck me as someone who had the potential to be a good general manager. He was Joe Sanchez, who had been a very successful salesman and had extensive experience in the service department of Xerox.

Joe was a bright, energetic, articulate, and confident fellow. He was not arrogant about his successes or being a Xerox employee, as so many seemed to be. He was a down-to-earth guy who was willing to listen. Joe wanted the job, but didn't demand or expect it because of who he was.

I gave Joe the general manager's job at Diablo, and told him the most important task he had was to get close to his OEM customers. I told him to get on a first name basis with the highest level in each client company. He had to make sure that these people knew that he, Joe Sanchez, was personally going to see that a good job was done, and that they could call him personally at any time, day or night.

Joe did exactly that! He was a master at it, and since he was success-driven, he made sure that the company performed. After all, it was his word on the line.

You must remember that in the OEM business, you don't have thousands of customers. In a $100 million business, you probably have less than 10 customers who represent 90 percent of your business, so it's not hard to get close to the client's top executive if you really try. These executives depend on you, and they typically spend several million dollars each year on your product. They appreciate top management attention.

Joe Sanchez did a good job at Diablo for the first couple of years. He actually made it profitable for a few quarters in 1982 and 1983, but unfortunately this didn't last. The company had done little to develop new products. Also, manufacturing costs were not competitive with offshore producers of printer products.

Xerox's method of product development had a great deal to do with Diablo's inability to get new products to market.

Diablo had invented the daisy wheel method of printing, which was more efficient, faster, and far less costly than band printers or even the IBM golf ball printer. It was a letter-quality printer and the base mechanism was perfect for a typewriter.

The corporate staff, Diablo, and Dallas operations had been planning a new product called Centaur, an electronic typewriter that would enter the 1 million unit per year market by 1981 or 1982. Because Diablo had the daisy wheel expertise, it was assumed that they would build the print mechanism, if not the entire machine.

Xerox's headquarters staff insisted that the development of Centaur should conform with the corporate Phase Review system. The Phase Review system was a product development procedure borrowed from IBM. The process was divided into phases; early phases would include stages such as design, prototype, and pre-production.

Before a product could advance from one phase to the next, a "Phase Review" involving all interested parties would be held. Representatives from each discipline, including sales, manufacturing, quality control, engineering, finance, and management, had to approve the completion of the current phase.

Anyone could reject the decision to continue, and require further study, tests or a redesign of the product. This would extend the product development time and increase costs.

This procedure sounds great in that it should prevent design errors or introduction of new products which cannot be easily or economically manufactured. The problem was that the process soon became "design by committee."

There were never-ending program reviews with Corporate and many arguments over development schedules, unit manufacturing costs, and distribution channels. The estimated product development costs for the Centaur became staggering, and the time to possible production became ridiculously long.

This was not surprising, for within Xerox, the average development time for a new copier in the early 1980s was *six years*!

I refused to impose this bureaucratic process on my other operations. We used good engineering practices, and conducted design reviews of cost goals, ease of manufacture, quality, and sales appeal with all concerned.

However, the general manager had the final say. There was no "veto" power, except his. Because of this, decisions were quick and timely.

The engineers and manufacturing people were expected to cooperate *and* perform their tasks properly. If they couldn't, then you needed different people. These people were critical to the operation, because the best phase review system in the world could not compensate for poor engineering.

Having chosen new leaders for Century Data and Diablo, there remained the most important operation of all in need of a leader: Dallas.

I did not want to leave the Dallas operations under XBS in El Segundo, even though I had great respect for Jim Campbell, who in early 1979 had been named as the newly-formed Xerox Business Systems chief, and became a Xerox Vice President.

Jim had been the highly successful head of Xerox Computer Services, a data services business that used the old SDS mainframes. He had previously been the founder of Greyhound Computer Services and earlier on, a successful salesman for IBM.

Jim is an easy going, bright, capable executive, always the gentleman, always helpful and eager to do a job. He was perfectly capable of running XBS as a group with good managers at Dallas and El Segundo.

However, I wanted Don Massaro at Dallas, and it was I, and not Kearns (as some people thought), who pushed for Don to be the new chief of Dallas. I wanted a "Pied Piper" in Dallas, and he was it. It didn't take much to convince Kearns or McColough, because they both liked Don very much. They also wanted Dallas to be successful and serve as an example of what a "new culture" could do for Xerox.

The idea of independent profit centers with entrepreneurial leaders to run fast-acting and responsive businesses was appealing. Both Kearns and McColough knew that the Xerox copier business had to change. It was getting mired in bureaucracy, inefficiency, and old-fashioned engineering, together with arrogance and complacency.

Another person who wanted to see Massaro in Dallas was Massaro. He wanted the job so badly he could taste it. So, in the summer of 1979, Don took over Dallas and away we went.

Don announced that Dallas would make a profit in less than a year. This was something that had never happened before, and few people believed would happen now.

But it did! With only the old line of word processors and a marginal performance line of facsimile machines, Dallas showed a modest profit in about 9 months. Don had cut costs, fired up the sales force, and increased revenue to a level slightly above breakeven.

Kearns, McColough, and I were very pleased. McColough gave me an "A" and put me on the Board of Directors at the May, 1980 shareholders meeting. Massaro was made a

Vice President and could do no wrong. Soon the halls at Stamford were full of whispered comments about Don being the next president of Xerox.

David Kearns had kept his word and put me on the Board of Directors. Now Jeanette and I attended all of the annual meetings and the many social functions associated with these occasions.

VII

XEROX: THE CULTURE

Jeanette became deeply involved with the church choir, church Outreach, and a local singing group named "The Park Street Singers." She had never seemed happier.

We both loved the church in New Canaan where Charlie Smith was pastor. Charlie had been the pastor of the Congregational Church for fifteen years and the congregation loved him.

Charlie was every bit as good as Ray Gaylord in Grand Rapids. He knew corporate life and its problems. I don't know how, but he delivered sermons that were right on the mark in dealing with every corporate frustration I had.

When I became head of the grounds committee, I was appalled to see the house provided to Charlie by the church. It was a large New England two-story house, but it was over 100 years old and was falling down. The inside was awful, with a leaky roof, cracked windows, and rotting sills.

I found out that the church had over $250,000 in liquid assets. In a very short time, I had authorized a complete renovation and remodeling of Charlie's house. It cost $50,000, which did not make me very popular with some of the old timers in the church.

In my opinion, it still was less than Charlie Smith and his wife deserved. To his credit, Charlie never had said anything to me about the poor condition of his home, but he thanked me afterwards with a bright twinkle in his eye.

Within two months of becoming general manager of the Dallas operation, Don Massaro had criticized every executive in Xerox's headquarters and copier operation. Even David Kearns didn't escape.

Don once told David, in front of his senior officers and Peter McColough, words to the effect that, "you can't run a business as big as copiers with no one having profit responsibility below the President and Chairman."

Another time, Don also said something like, "Kearns, you gotta kick some butt out there, the Japanese are eating your lunch and those guys in BPG (Business Products Group) don't even know it!"

And: "None of those guys at Rochester ever ran anything—break it up and put some professional general managers in there with profit responsibility, pay them big if they do the job, fire them if they don't."

David knew Don was right, but he didn't know what to do when virtually every executive in Xerox, including those in Stamford, was against changing the structure. Almost all hated Don, who certainly wasn't endearing himself to them.

Don was the opposite of everything the corporate staff culture respected. The staff was dignified, quiet, bureaucratic, protective, cautious, staff-dependent, and politically-oriented. Don, however, was flashy, boisterous, entrepreneurial, open, "full speed ahead," decisive, and couldn't care less about politics.

The meetings that Don attended in Stamford were at a level where many types of people participated: strategic planners, research, finance, Business Products Group staffers, and sales people. They always looked for something wrong with Don's presentations.

At one meeting, Don gave one of his usually compelling and convincing presentations. I don't recall the project that was being discussed, but no doubt it was something costly which needed corporate approval. Don probably already had it in effect, and would continue it regardless of the corporate position.

When he finished his speech, no one said a word for several seconds. Then, one of the high-level executives made a condescending comment: "Good presentation, Don. This looks like a program we should study for the future."

Don looked at him and said, "Jack, you're an asshole!"

People all over the room sucked in their breath. David couldn't let even Don get away with that in front of all of those people, so he said, "Don, we don't act that way in these meetings. I want you to apologize to Jack immediately."

Delight arose in the faces of Don's enemies, who included just about everyone in the room. Don calmly walked over to the offended executive, put his hand on his shoulder and said, "Jack, I'm sorry you're an asshole!"

With Dallas on the way to recovery, I decided it was time to give the Star/Ethernet project to Don Massaro. The project was headed by David Liddle, a brilliant engineer and manager who had worked at the research center on ALTO, the code name for the PARC-developed networked personal computer product.

It was at PARC that the Ethernet network and systems software were developed. This research included pioneering work on the currently popular "mouse" that is used for cursor operation and the selection of "windowed" screens and icons.

Liddle had undertaken the task of making this research marketable.

ALTO had become a product and was put into networks throughout Xerox worldwide. Every Xerox business in the world, including headquarters, had an ALTO system connected via Ethernet locally, and was connected nationally and internationally via the phone system.

It provided a great system for word processing, publishing, communications, and office filing. It was an "office of the future" product, although it was a prototype and therefore not yet suitable for full production.

ALTO was expensive by personal computer standards; of course, it wasn't a personal computer. It was far more. ALTO could do everything a personal computer could, but it was also a networked system that provided high-speed communications between terminals. The system offered electronic mail and interactive messaging. High-speed laser printers were shared in the system. When I talked about ALTO to other people, I made an analogy with an Apple computer, in that having an Apple was like having *one* telephone in a system that had no other telephones connected to it.

Unfortunately, the media and consulting sages of industry couldn't see beyond the product's "tube." They also compared ALTO to the Apple, but without much perception of ALTO's potential. Essentially, the Apple at that time wasn't much more than a toy.

In my opinion, Xerox had made a mistake in the decision to abandon ALTO in favor of a new replacement project called STAR. While the new project was necessary and important in the long term, abandoning ALTO took Xerox out of the office system market. This also put serious time pressures on the new STAR program.

Liddle was convinced that he could make STAR better and cheaper than ALTO, which was designed in the mid-1970s. He started from scratch in building the hardware and software. However, we simply did not have enough time to finish the development of the product *and* meet our ambitious marketing schedule.

The project never was finished, even when it was introduced in 1981. Had we improved ALTO and introduced STAR later, we might have had a better chance for success in office systems.

When Don Massaro first was introduced to STAR, he wanted to kill the project. He thought it was a research "pipe dream." After he met Liddle and listened to him, Don decided that STAR would revolutionize the way businesses were operated. He thought it was the greatest product he had ever seen.

This was partly because David Liddle is the most articulate communicator of technical information I have ever met. Also, Don had the vision to see that a "Macintosh" product which was networked to allow stored data to be shared, documents to be transmitted in seconds across the room or across the nation, and data to be electronically filed and accessed in seconds, would be a clear winner.

Such a product would need terminals, electronic typewriters, laser printers, floppy disks, hard disks, network software, and a document reader. Xerox owned all this technology! Shugart made floppy disks, Century Data made hard disks, El Segundo made laser printers, Diablo made daisy wheel printers, Dallas made terminals and typewriters: *we had it all!*

We merely needed to put together a program to sell these systems. This would involve leveraging as much as possible the great copier sales organization, which had a force 10,000 strong in the U.S. alone.

So why didn't Xerox enjoy great success in office systems? In my opinion, there are several reasons, any one of which might have brought failure.

By the late 1970s, the Xerox Corporation had become bureaucratic and finance-oriented. It had lost its technological lead in copiers partly because it had isolated its engineers from customers and reality for years. The engineers did not know what the customers wanted.

The *sales organization* had the responsibility for recording profits. They paid only the manufacturing costs for products, and subsequently set prices for leasing and sales. The consolidation of financials that included corporate and engineering costs occurred within the corporate books.

Up until the early 1980s, copier prices had no relationship to their costs because there was little or no competition. Xerox assigned high prices to their products and watched the profits roll in. When the competition started to become a problem, the sales management sold off the equipment used for leasing to meet their targeted profits.

Because of their "success," the sales division became arrogant as well as bureaucratic.

When Dallas came out with the world's second personal computer after Apple, called the Model 820 personal computer, the obvious distribution outlet was through the 10,000 salesmen in the copier organization. Since my organization was considered an independent profit center, we wanted the sales force to sell with a commission incentive. We also would pay the sales overhead, but Dallas would obviously record the profits or losses.

The management of the Business Product Group (BPG), the copier sales organization, *refused* to sell the product if they could not record the profits! They also objected to the product because it had not been developed under the "Phase Review" process used by the copier organization.

Originally, this product had been named SAM. According to Don Massaro, it was named after *me*, having used my "Sam" Titsworth story at an employees' meeting. It officially stood for "Simply Amazing Machine."

Dallas had quite an advertising program planned for it, including television ads in which a Humphrey Bogart character said, "Play it again, SAM." Corporate staff thought this was all very unsophisticated, and said we had to call it the Model 820 personal computer.

IBM had entered the personal computer business at precisely the same time we had. IBM had announced a 16-bit system, while the Model 820 was an 8-bit system. The copier sales force was convinced that our system therefore would not sell. The fact that the two available Apple personal computers were 8-bit products and selling like hot cakes didn't matter.

The Xerox sales organization and the corporation had become a commodity product organization. They sold copiers in very much the same way as Procter and Gamble sold soap or General Mills sold cereal.

Technical knowledge hardly entered the sales picture, so most salesmen selling copiers were not knowledgeable enough to handle a situation involving personal computers.

Nobody at headquarters understood much about technology. I never considered myself a technical person, especially in computers, but I was more knowledgeable than most of my associates, especially the Board of Directors.

This reminds me of the time I showed a movie about STAR at a Board of Directors' meeting in 1982. The movie was of "home" version quality, made by Liddle's people to show internally. It was ten minutes long, and demonstrated the "in-house" publishing capability of the STAR network.

The film featured the screen of a computer that displayed icons used to select functions such as filing (picture of a file cabinet) or printing (picture of a printer). When an icon was selected, the computer's screen would show text with tables, sketches, and pictures. The film showed that the screen images could be moved to different locations on the screen by manipulating the cursor with a "mouse." The computer's operator was shown selecting the print icon, and the exact image on the screen came out of a networked laser printer in hard copy.

I thought this film would not be too difficult to follow! I had shown the film previously to David Kearns and asked him if he thought it would be of interest to the Board. I explained that the film had not been professionally produced, but I would follow this movie with an explanation to the Board.

David thought it would be a good idea.

The film was shown on our big screen in the Board room and afterwards I stood up to make my comments. Before I could speak, the booming voice of one of our outside directors said: "What the hell was that?"

I said, "I'm sorry, what do you mean?"

The same question was repeated, very indignantly and loudly: "What the hell was that?"

I said, "That was our new STAR product."

Again: "What the hell was that! That was the worst movie I've ever seen—it told me nothing. I don't know what I saw!"

The final insult came from another outside director, who said rather indignantly, "Next time, use some decent music— that was just California hippie music!"

I admit that the movie clearly was not self-explanatory, and I should have realized that some people wouldn't understand even basic technology. I'm usually very good at playing to my audience, but clearly I had failed this time. I could accept that.

What I couldn't accept was the contempt and abuse that came from these men.

I initially was shocked and petrified at this outbreak, but later I was absolutely furious. These people were completely insensitive to the impact their contemptuous comments made on me, on the other members of the Board, and on the project itself.

It is interesting that without my knowledge someone later commissioned a professional group to make a movie for the Board about Xerox's new products and its dedication to "non-copier" businesses. It was a great piece of work; it cost $200,000 and featured all of the top managers, except me. It had pictures of Xerox's buildings, the waterfall outside headquarters, images of the new products, and *soft* music.

The movie was shown at our Board meeting in Vienna in late 1982, and received no negative remarks. The movie required no thought on the part of the audience.

The really sad part of this incident wasn't the humiliation and the "put-down" I endured, but the fact that these men were looking at a "Macintosh" years before Apple came out with that product. They wouldn't show the interest or take the time to understand what it was and could mean to the company.

The fact that I may have made an inadequate presentation should have prompted a desire on their part to know more. Instead, they were satisfied to show contempt of me for having "wasted their time."

It is not that one needs absolute support from a corporate Board to bring out a new product, but when others in the company are looking for reasons to discontinue new efforts, such vociferous negative responses from the highest level doesn't enhance one's ability to move forward.

Perhaps I am naive in believing that all corporate Board members should familiarize themselves with the people, products, and programs of their company. I find that some Board members are there because their names read well in the proxy statement.

Perhaps I was too sensitive. Bob Price at CDC once told me that I "couldn't distinguish between a flea bite and a snake bite." This may not have been a snake bite, but it certainly was an infestation of fleas.

Since we did not sell the Model 820 personal computer through our copier sales force, IPG set up its own distributors and dealers. The sales force in the Dallas division was too small to sell directly to the public. They were needed to work on a full-time basis with dealers and distributors, if we were to achieve any reasonable volume.

We started to move products through dealers in 1981, and had the kind of problems you would expect with a new product. Fortunately, there was nothing we could not overcome with a few fixes.

The biggest problem was the "apparent" limitation of software that used the CPM operating system, which was our base system software. CPM had been selected because it was an industry standard, and it saved us time and money in that we did not have to develop our own operating system and applications. Applications software came from outside devel-opers; in fact, we had more of such programs than IBM.

These applications included Wordstar for word process-ing, as well as other programs for things like spreadsheets. Word processing and spreadsheets represented 95 percent of the use of personal computers.

Even though there wasn't a real problem, our competi-tion made points with our customers on the "software limita-tions" of the Model 820.

One can't overlook the impact that IBM had on Xerox programs. At one of our corporate review sessions, Don Massaro had been asked what was the worst thing that could happen to the Xerox personal computer project.

Don replied: "If IBM announces a personal computer with newer technology at about the same time that we an-nounce our personal computer, and also sells them through retail stores, we're in real trouble." That is exactly what IBM did.

To top it off, the copier sales force demanded that IPG not use dealers in office equipment for our personal computer if those dealers also sold non-Xerox copiers such as Canon, Sharp, and Savin. This was an outrageous demand, because no dealer sold Xerox copiers. The copier sales force sold directly to the public.

Since almost all good office equipment dealers sold non-Xerox copiers, we would have been left with the few bad ones. Corporate management ultimately overruled the copier sales people, but Xerox didn't do well in the small personal computer business.

There is no doubt in my mind that the Xerox personal computer could have been a success if the copier sales force had supported the product, even with IBM's entry into the market. Subsequent generations of this product would have taken us to a Macintosh-like product long before Apple had time to use the Xerox technology for that unit.

Having learned our lesson with the personal computer, Don Massaro and I were determined to make the Centaur electronic typewriter program successful. This project was being run at both Diablo *and* Dallas.

Dallas had contracted with a group in Chicago, a small shop with an entrepreneurial leader and six technicians and engineers, who we called the "Chicago Seven." They were determined to develop an electronic typewriter, using daisy wheel technology, that would outperform the IBM golfball unit and which could be made for less than $300 in the U.S.

To achieve such a production cost, for a unit which could be sold for over $1,000, was considered impossible by everyone in Xerox, except Don and the Chicago Seven.

Diablo had the capability to develop such a product and already was working on it. However, they were approaching the task at a snail's pace, constantly re-starting after corporate staff reviews. It would have taken forever for Diablo to finish this product, and I doubt that the cost targets would have been met.

I made a very unpopular decision to support Don. One reason I supported him was that he and his people talked about how they would meet our design and cost goals. The people at Diablo and Corporate spent their time talking about why they *could not* meet our design and cost goals.

Dallas proceeded with the project and went to the copier sales force, with hat in hand, and said, "It's yours. You sell it, you can have the profits. We'll transfer the unit to you at manufacturing cost, not including engineering overhead and other costs, which we at IPG will absorb."

Dallas built the Memorywriter (the new name for Centaur) locally and used a revolutionary approach to its manufacture. In 1982, they started the first "just in time" inventory system and built a fully automated factory.

The facility had been a small warehouse on the outskirts of Dallas. It was converted to house an automated assembly line, with parts arriving within hours of their use.

When it was up and running full steam, we made typewriters with less than 40 minutes of labor and with a total cost of under $300. We had the capacity to make over 300,000 typewriters per year. Our tooling costs, including automation, was under $10 million and the project development was done in 18 months for under $5 million.

Xerox had never developed a copier in less than five years, and usually did so at staggering costs. I recall that before the Series 10 copier was introduced in 1983, the negative cash flow was several hundred million dollars!

With the Memorywriter, the copier sales force had its first non-copier product and marketed it successfully with the same commodity product approach used with copiers. They were so successful that in less than 18 months, Xerox matched IBM's market share in the electronic typewriter marketplace.

We transferred the unit to BPG at manufacturing cost. As agreed, IPG ate the overhead and engineering costs, and, of course, reported a loss on the project from then on.

In the copier "cigar box" accounting system, the startup costs for the Memorywriter were budgeted and absorbed along with the incredible development and launch costs of other Xerox products. With the continuing sell-off of the lease base, the Xerox copier business continued to show a profit.

IPG, on the other hand, continued to show losses, since we did not receive revenue or profits from the Memorywriter. Decreasing revenue from the Model 820 personal computer and high development costs for the STAR "office of the future" network system made IPG's bottom line appear even worse.

On top of these problems, BPG was demanding a "single sales force" for the entire corporation. Essentially, the copier organization wanted to sell and record the profits for all products of the company, which included copiers, typewriters, and personal computers.

In addition, they proposed to buy personal computers for resale to customers from someone other than Xerox Dallas. BPG supported a spinoff group of dissidents from Dallas that was developing a product that Don and I had discontinued. They proposed to sell the STAR network systems as well.

The copier sales force was made up of people who had sold primarily door-to-door, supported by expensive national advertising programs. Their pricing strategy was based on how much profit was necessary, and was not related to cost because there had been no competition.

Selling a complex computer network doesn't work on a "calls per week" approach, a standard with which the sales force was familiar. Getting an order for a million-dollar system was measured in months, and was not related to how many calls were required of a salesman each week. This new orientation surely was confusing and frustrating to most of the copier sales force.

I actually favored a single sales force because I think it is the only way one can properly manage sales resources when one is selling a broad product line. *One* organization should manage the major accounts and geographic areas and be responsible for sales quotas for all products.

However, I did not believe that this sales organization should be *responsible for profit*. The profit responsibility and the *marketing* function should stay with the operational unit. The single *field* sales organization should be a "quota/expense" organization.

It always has been my philosophy that salesmen should *sell* and businessmen should *manage* the business.

A strong sales-oriented person with an engineering, manufacturing, and finance background should lead an operation of *manageable* size with responsibility for engineering, manufacturing, finance, and marketing. "Marketing," in this context, includes product planning, pricing, advertising, and any other sales function except direct selling and order/collection administration activities.

Besides the obvious problem of the copier sales force's inability to sell complex systems, IPG would be required to transfer to BPG *all* our products at manufacturing cost and forego revenue and profits. We would become a cost center, but as we were required to report to Corporate as a profit center, we would always show a loss. Eventually, we would report as a cost center.

This is hardly the way to provide incentive to progressive, entrepreneurial, risk-taking, non-bureaucratic managers. As I recall writing in a memo to the copier people, "No red-blooded American entrepreneur will be happy running a cost center—it has a negative connotation."

I decided to work towards the goal of a single sales force, but to do it in a planned and careful manner. I proposed a phased approach, starting with simple products like facsimile. IPG would transfer STAR systems sales only after Dallas had some initial marketing success with that product.

However, Don Massaro wasn't interested in running an operation which didn't include sales. The copier people were not willing to wait; they wanted the responsibility immediately and would take care of any problems that arose. Everybody therefore nominally accepted my "phased" single sales force proposals, but didn't take them seriously.

In the middle of all this corporate frustration, there were some good things happening to Jeanette and me. In 1980, I had received my annual solicitation for a contribution to my alma mater, the Rose-Hulman Institute of Technology. As usual, I wrote a check for $100 and sent it off to the school.

Shortly afterwards, I received a *glowing* thank-you note that was personally signed by Dr. Sam Hulbert, President of Rose-Hulman. While the letter was in good taste, it was obvious to me that it said, in effect: "How can someone making several hundred thousand dollars a year be so unaware of the needs of his alma mater?" As I recall, I then sent a check for something like $1,000 to the school.

A few months later, I received a call from Dr. Hulbert. He asked me how long it had been since I had visited the campus. When I told Sam I hadn't been back since graduation, he said he thought he had a way to get me there. He then informed me that the Board of Rose-Hulman had awarded me an Honorary Doctorate in Engineering.

I must say that the event almost overwhelmed me. I never expected such an honor. It certainly bolstered my self-esteem, and compensated greatly for the less satisfying events then occurring in my business career.

Early in 1981, we made a decision to announce the debut of the STAR system. We at Xerox, along with the media *and* the people in industry who would use "office of the future" products, were all caught up in our own hype. All of the potential suppliers, including Wang, Xerox, IBM, Apple, DEC, and hordes of newcomers, were being reported by analysts and media people to be on the verge of releasing bold new futuristic products into a $300 billion per year office automation market.

As usual, the marketing people were talking about the narrow "window" of opportunity; if you were not on the cutting edge, all would be lost.

We at IPG knew we were not *quite* ready to go into full production, so we decided to announce that our STAR network product was in a test marketing program. We wanted to limit sales to a select group of Fortune 500 companies. In the meantime, we would complete our applications software and improve our operating system software as bugs were identified in the field.

It was a risky but not a wild plan. I received from David Liddle a framed, hand-painted sketch of a STAR network system with the caption, "The toothpaste is out of the tube— thanks for your support of STAR."

Well, the paste was certainly out of the tube and it would be impossible to put it back in.

As one might expect when rushing a product to market, there were many technical problems. The most serious of these problems was that the operating system software severely limited the response time of the computer. Communications was one of the great features of the STAR network, yet the system was very slow.

Another major problem was related to the timing of our introduction of the product to the market place. We were not late entering the market, we were far too early.

No customer, except a few of the entrepreneurial "lunatic fringe" who wanted to experiment, was ready to change the way it did business. This Xerox product practically abolished paper systems and created a digital electronic system in its place.

It's ironic that such a system, if it were truly successful, would eliminate the need for plain paper office copiers. Incidentally, this will happen during the next one or two decades, something I predicted to the copier people when I was at Xerox. It was a very unpopular view.

I found out that it is one thing to "create" a market. However, it is another matter entirely to create a market *and* fundamentally change the environment in which business is conducted. We were trying to change the way people communicate and do business with each other. A commitment from a customer to this new environment is not trivial.

To overhaul its operations, a customer would have to buy multiple copies of our business systems product. The lowest price for *one* of our office systems was $100,000, and very often a customer would pay upwards of $1 million when revamping its operations. I estimated that for General Electric to automate its entire national office structure, its systems purchase costs would be in excess of $100 million.

Niccolo di Bernardo Machiavelli (1469-1527), the Florentine court advisor, once said:

> "It must be realized that there is nothing more difficult to plan, more uncertain of success or more dangerous to manage than the establishment of a new order of things; for he who introduces it makes enemies of all those who derived advantage from the old order and find but lukewarm defenders among those who stand to gain from the new one. Such a lukewarm attitude grows from the incredulity of men in general who actually have no faith in new things until they have been proven by experience."

While that incredible statement was made 470 years earlier, it was absolutely the problem confronting Xerox in 1980. The STAR product offered a complete solution to a problem at a time when the customer was hardly ready for a *partial* solution.

Don and his people were so close to the "answer", and could see the benefit of networked computers so clearly that they wouldn't listen to the customers or me. They built up the organization to sell Ethernet and the STAR system as a generic solution to office inefficiency.

I understood their position and also believed their approach may have been correct, except for their timing. I didn't think the product was ready for mass distribution, and the cash requirements for a broad market introduction would be unaffordable.

I knew that Xerox was starting to feel the crunch of Japanese competition in the copier business. Also, Xerox's lack of available cash for the first time was becoming a problem.

Massaro and Liddle had projected several hundred million dollars in revenue for 1982, 1983, and 1984. However, they had missed their 1981 forecast by several million dollars in revenue. I saw nothing in their new plan that adjusted for those results.

I wanted to enter specific niche markets, such as "in-house" publishing. Dallas was gearing up to mass-produce a concept (networked personal computers) that was not yet accepted.

I wrote a memo to Massaro and Liddle about Xerox's cash problem. In it, I *ordered* them to change their long-range plan to a more realistic approach that targeted niche markets for the STAR/Ethernet systems.

The memo came back to me with the stamped imprint: "THIS IDEA STINKS—DON MASSARO."

Well, that did it for me. I got the returned memo about 4:00 p.m. Eastern time and told my chief financial officer,

Walter Kirson, that as soon as I could find Don, I would fire him.

I couldn't find Don, because Walter got to him first and told him to "disappear until John cooled off." Then, Walter convinced me that firing Don on the spot would create all kinds of problems for the company, especially with the media, who loved our maverick leader in Dallas.

Fortune had written a long cover story article on Massaro and Xerox in May, 1982, and this was August. It was a very complimentary article, with an interesting ending:

> "It looks as though Xerox's top managers are using Massaro and his crew to peddle change to the rest of the corporation. Any such project doubtless irritates some powerful corporate staffers, so Massaro's first mistake could be his last."

I cooled off and Don offered me his profound apologies. He stated that he thought some corporate staffer had written the memo for me. He probably did think so, because this was the first time I had not supported him completely. I didn't think the memo was that bad, but maybe by then the bureaucracy was getting to me!

I refused to approve the Dallas budget and said so to David Kearns. I told him that it was unachievable, but that Don probably would not change it. I suggested to David that he might want to go to Dallas without me and decide for himself.

David went to Dallas and reviewed the 1983 plan with Massaro and Liddle. When he came back to Stamford, David told me to go with the plan "as is." He actually had little choice, since things were pretty much "cast in concrete" by then.

Massaro and Liddle resigned from Xerox in the fall of 1982. They were convinced, as was I, that a single sales force run by the copier division could never successfully sell the network computer systems products. Time has proven that we were correct.

The other businesses in Xerox weren't faring too well in 1982, either. The cash crunch prompted me to look closely at all operations.

I had been given the Western Union International Corporation (WUI), headed by Ed Gallager. It was to become part of Xerox's worldwide communication services business and included the XTEN project.

XTEN was Abe Zarem's contribution to Xerox's future success in communications. In the 1960s, Abe Zarem had been a member of the Board of Directors at Xerox. Xerox had acquired the Electro Optics Corporation, which Abe had founded and run.

Abe subsequently left the Board and became a high-level Xerox employee responsible for setting up the Xerox Venture Capital division. He also was responsible for acquisitions, which included Versatec, Shugart, and Century Data, and special projects such as XTEN.

XTEN was a project of great magnitude and ambition in that it planned to make Xerox eventually surpass both IBM and AT&T in the communications industry.

I had a five-year cash flow study done for the XTEN project in 1982. The study showed a negative cash flow of several billion dollars over the next five years. When I showed this to Peter McColough, we canceled XTEN the very next day.

Afterwards, WUI made no strategic sense to Xerox, so I got approval to sell the company. We accomplished that in about six months, when MCI bought WUI. The price was good for MCI, and made a nice profit for Xerox.

I decided shortly thereafter that we should consider selling some other IPG assets such as Shugart, Century Data, and possibly Diablo. I had a valuation and market study done by Mitchell and Company, which showed a possible sales value of over $500 million for all three businesses. Shugart, with an annual revenue of several hundred million dollars and substantial profits, was clearly the most valuable.

We started a quiet "unofficial" project on the West Coast to determine interest in Shugart. Shugart was doing well in 1982 and 1983, but it was clear that the company couldn't stay competitive unless a large part of the labor was done offshore in Taiwan, Singapore, or Hong Kong.

There was no way the Xerox copier union would stand for such a move. They had agreed not to organize Shugart, but that deal didn't include sending jobs to the Far East. I never liked that prospect either, but it was clear that Shugart would go downhill if offshore production were not implemented.

I concluded that since Xerox couldn't save Shugart, let someone else do it! I went looking for buyers, and I found one in a fairly new but high-flying company called Seagate, Al Shugart's new company.

Finis Connor, a Seagate founder and director, through Don Massaro suggested a purchase price for Shugart of $300 million. About two-thirds of the offer was made up of Seagate stock.

The Xerox corporate staff considered the offer ridiculous, because they thought Seagate stock was "worthless." Also, since we had just sold WUI, they thought it was inappropriate to appear as if Xerox were "dumping" its assets.

Incredible! We might not have received $300 million from Seagate in the end, but $250 million was very possible.

Instead, Xerox kept Shugart and didn't move its manufacturing offshore. Shugart revenue and profits declined to the point that Xerox practically gave it away after several million dollars were lost. Seagate grew to over $2 billion in revenue and its "worthless" stock tripled in value.

It was obvious in April, 1983, that the Dallas operation was doomed. The other IPG subsidiaries, except for Shugart and Versatec (always a winner, in great part due to Zaphiropoulos), were going nowhere but down. The bureaucracy at Diablo, the poor technical position of Century Data, the less than successful introduction of STAR/Ethernet, the personal computer marketing fiasco and the resignation of Massaro at Dallas, together with a declining cash position at Xerox, spelled real trouble.

With the 1981 shortfall in profits in Dallas, the corporate staff had its "opportunity" to get back in control. I must say it was hard to argue that a $100 million profit shortfall did not warrant some corporate attention.

The irony of it all was that a $100 million *investment* in the network systems business was reasonable. If Dallas had budgeted such a loss for 1981, it very likely would have been approved. Compared to the tremendous costs incurred in developing and introducing the new Series 10 copier, or the several hundred million dollar losses *budgeted* for the 9200 laser printer, our "investment" in the "office of the future" was a relatively small amount of money.

The good news was that the Memorywriter was a success. Xerox eventually captured about 30 percent of the high-end typewriter market. Unfortunately, this success did not appear in the Dallas or IPG financial statements. The copier sales organization received the profits for this product.

The corporate finance office would not be convinced to establish a reporting system that gave credit for profits by product line to the originating development and manufacturing division. Since profits had always been recorded and credited to the copier sales division, the finance office wouldn't change the process.

This was an extremely frustrating situation.

Missing a budget by several million dollars could not be condoned by me or anyone else. The corporate strategists, staff engineers, finance officers, quality control group, and facilities managers each had ideas of how to solve the problem.

Of course, the copier sales organization got their single sales force program under way.

Shelby Carter was assigned to me as an assistant group executive to "help" me "stop the bleeding" at Dallas.

Shelby was an extremely bright and highly confident executive. He was the quintessential salesman, and the field representatives loved him. I liked Shelby and had asked Kearns to assign him to me.

With or without Shelby's help, it was far too late in 1983 to get the IPG businesses on track. Except for Versatec and Shugart, it may have been too late when I had joined Xerox four years earlier.

Looking back, a way to have salvaged the situation might have been to have closed Dallas shortly after I came in and then implemented the next-generation typewriter program at Diablo. That might have saved Diablo, although I question whether or not the Diablo and corporate staff approach would have resulted in a successful typewriter product. We also could have delayed STAR and introduced it more cautiously.

It was not my nature to "give up", but I must say there are times when retreat is the better part of valor.

In January, 1983, I made a presentation to about 200 Xerox senior managers, including people from Rank Xerox, Fuji Xerox, and others from around the world. This was part of a program where each major division head was to present his strategy.

I chose to talk about my businesses in the context of the entire company. I wanted to show that it all made strategic sense, and that everything could fit together if we just had the courage, patience and dedication to go forward.

I talked about the resources Xerox had; that we had all the technology and products to be an "office systems" company. I talked about how Xerox was a success because of technology and that we needed to keep the proper emphasis on technology. I ended with a plea for support of the office systems business.

After the conclusion of this presentation, I asked for questions and discussion. I got *one comment* from a Rank Xerox executive. It was the *only* response to what I considered to be a presentation that for the first time covered a broad and rather complete strategic view of the future of Xerox Corporation.

Shortly after this planning meeting, the chief financial officer, Mel Howard, convinced Kearns and McColough to buy Crum and Forster, a multi-billion dollar liability insurance company. In my opinion, that was the beginning of the end for Xerox in technology products other than copiers.

Because the speech that I had given in early 1983 about how Xerox had everything it took to be the leader in office automation was less than enthusiastically embraced, I soon afterwards started thinking about leaving Xerox. It was an agonizing period for me, because I couldn't avoid also feeling like a "quitter," or worse, like a failure. This was not a good way to end an otherwise highly successful career.

At this time I was 59 years old, only one year away from the mandatory age of retirement for senior company officers. However, I was old enough to meet the 55 year minimum retirement age. As I had private luncheons with David Kearns on a routine basis, I decided to suggest the possibility of my retirement to David at the next occasion.

It was ironic that according to the public relations office, my presentation at the planning meeting was the best overall strategy for Xerox they had ever seen. It also had impressed David, and he told me at our luncheon that he had seriously considered making me the chief strategy officer of Xerox. The problem was that the copier people would never have accepted me in that role.

I knew David wanted to re-organize the company, and I had correctly guessed that he was having difficulty in deciding where I could best serve Xerox. I think I could have been a real asset to Xerox as its chief strategy officer, but I understand why David couldn't make that move.

David and I decided that I would retire in mid-1983. At that time, the restructuring of Xerox would be completed.

In the process of leaving Xerox, I made recommendations on who should take my place. I strongly urged that Paul Allaire be given my job, since he was returning from Rank Xerox as managing director, with a great success to his credit.

Paul clearly knew the copier business, so my old job offered him the opportunity to learn about the other major part of the company. He was extremely capable, which would give Xerox the best chance to make something of STAR/Ethernet.

Paul was being groomed for the presidency and I thought this would broaden him for that job. To my surprise, Paul was given the job of chief staff officer.

When I asked the personnel department why he hadn't been given my old job, they said: "There is too much risk for Paul in that job. We want him to be the next president and we don't want his career tainted, which is very likely in IPG. We'll get someone from outside the copier company for that job."

I thought to myself, "You mean someone like good old Johnny T!"

VIII

VENTURES IN NON-RETIREMENT

In May, 1983, around the time when I decided to retire from Xerox, a pleasant event occurred. The President of one of the local banks in my home town of Robinson, Illinois, called to tell me I had been selected to be honored by the local agribusiness association and the community. It was a "home town boy makes good" event.

The bank invited 500 people from the city and county to a nice dinner. Dinner was followed by several prominent citizens listing my accomplishments and titles, which included being sole director of five multimillion dollar U.S. corporations, all owned by Xerox.

I was then presented with a membership to the local country club, a fine golf bag, and other nice gifts. Many of my high school friends were there, along with a number of my relatives.

My mother sat in the front row, and was as proud as she could be. I wished that my father had lived so that he could have been there. He would not have said much, but it would have been a great day for him.

That evening, there was a drawing for a cash prize of $100. Each of the guests had put their names in a box. Jeanette was asked to make the drawing. She pulled out a name, and then asked to draw another. She had drawn my name the first time! When things go well, everything goes well. Jeanette had asked earlier for our names not to be put in the drawing, because it clearly would have been embarrassing for us to win.

I took that occasion to announce my retirement from Xerox. I had decided to join a venture capital company that was headed by my good friend and neighbor in New Canaan, Bob Williams.

Bob and Ginny Williams lived across the street. They were great friends who had relatively young children; these children were almost young enough to be our grandchildren.

Bob and I had become golfing buddies, and knew each other well. Bob's grandfather had founded Tampax Corporation, and Bob's father had been the Board Chairman of that corporation. Bob was on the Board of Directors, and had voting control of the family interests.

You would think someone with that background would be financially secure, but for some reason that Bob didn't understand, his father had never given him substantial funds. Bob had made his own way as an accounting and finance executive.

Bob had been head of the venture capital operation of a major corporation before he moved to New Canaan in 1979. He formed Regional Financial Enterprises (RFE) in 1980, after raising $10 million from bank holding companies around the Midwest and East Coast.

When Bob found out that I was leaving Xerox, he proposed that I join him as a general partner in a new venture fund that he was in the process of raising.

Venture capital companies typically solicit investments from corporations, state and corporate retirement funds, bank holding companies, insurance companies, and occasionally, individuals. The venture fund is made up of these cumulative investments, and is targeted at a specific total amount, perhaps $40 or $50 million.

The general partners of the venture company then invest those funds in relatively high risk ventures, such as start-up companies in high tech businesses. The investors become limited partners in the venture company.

Venture capital companies like RFE make their money from charging a fee for managing the limited partners' money, and by taking a percentage of the profits made (usually 20 percent) when the investments mature.

The most famous venture-backed start-up company was Apple Computer. A few million dollars invested in starting Apple Computer grew to tens of millions when Apple went public.

Actually, venture capital companies did not own a very large percentage of Apple Computer stock.

The Xerox Venture Capital Fund, under Abe Zarem, invested a relatively small amount of money in Apple. This occurred after Don Massaro, a friend of Apple's founder, Steve Jobs, had twisted Abe's arm. From that investment, Xerox received several million dollars when Apple went public.

To Steve Jobs, the small investment that he received from Xerox may have been worth millions of dollars to Apple. That investment gave Steve access to Xerox's PARC, where he saw the STAR technology.

In the late 1970s and early 1980s, there were many stories of incredible profits made by venture companies who had backed high tech companies that were in the computer business. Such computer operations included: Apple, Cray Research, Network Systems, Versatec, Shugart, and Microsoft.

The Federal government had lowered the capital gains tax, so there was a rush to form venture capital funds. Everyone planned to get in on the "gravy train."

I had introduced Bob Williams to Dr. Bob Sparacino, who had been Xerox's chief engineer and later my technical staff vice president. Sparacino had just retired from Xerox.

A brilliant technologist, Sparacino seemed a natural for venture capital. Williams made Sparacino and me general partners in RFE II (the second fund), which was closed in late 1983. This fund had notable investors, including Prudential, IBM, Weyerhauser, the Northwest Bank of Minneapolis, and the State of Michigan pension fund.

Unfortunately, almost all funds formed in the middle 1980s didn't do well. The overall market situation at the time was such that there were so many venture funds that money was almost *thrown* at any entrepreneur or technologist who hinted at a technical idea.

Too many general partners in these new venture capital companies were young, inexperienced business school graduates in their 20s and 30s. They didn't understand the management of companies and they had no patience with the development schedules of high tech products.

When a technical problem occurred in the development process, which was often, the general partners' inclination, and too often their action, was to fire the company president, who was almost always the technologist or inventor.

Among high tech development companies, one could expect three or four out of five to fail under the best conditions. The immature approach to managing companies almost guaranteed five out of five failures.

Unfortunately, our fund was not immune from some of these same problems. I was on the Board of Directors of one company with several of these "whiz kids" where we had three presidents in less than 18 months.

I tried to impress upon these people the difficulty and the time required to develop new innovative products. I usually gave them a list that showed the development history of a number of well-known products:

Time Span from Date of Invention to a Marketable Product

Ball Point Pen	1938-1945	7 years
Instant Camera	1945-1947	2 years
Instant Coffee	1934-1956	22 years
Gyro Compass	1852-1908	56 years
Fluorescent Light	1901-1934	33 years
Magnetic Recording	1900-1937	37 years
Radio	1890-1914	24 years
Transistor	1940-1958	18 years
Xerox Copier	1935-1950	15 years
Zipper	1883-1913	30 years

It didn't matter. Most venture companies wanted to see big successes and returns in two to three years. I felt such people were in the wrong business. I once commented that venture capital people are the least venturesome people I've ever known. Most of them would do well performing leveraged buyouts.

Bob Sparacino and I left in 1986 as general partners in RFE. I'm sure we were a great disappointment to Bob Williams, but he since has managed to continue with RFE funds III and IV by concentrating on less high tech investments, such as health care.

I think venture capital is very important to developing new high tech products and services. Everything from genetic engineering and medical products, to computers and services such as Federal Express, has needed that financial backing. The major problem has been (as it is so often), that people get involved with businesses they don't understand.

It doesn't matter whether the business is venture capital, insurance, or computers; if you don't stick with what you do best, you probably won't do it well! There are some venture companies, such as Norwest Venture, who are truly knowledgeable and competent in technology chosen fields. I would urge those companies and pension funds which typically invest in venture capital to continue to do so, but with prudence.

From my business experiences on the East Coast, one might surmise that we didn't care for that part of the country. Not so! We loved New Canaan and made many dear friends during our seven years there.

I loved the big house with its three acres of lawn, trees, and many flower gardens. I knew every oak, maple, pine, black walnut, and beech. We even had a Portuguese cork tree, a magnificent specimen. I vowed never to sell the place.

One Sunday, I was outside the Congregational Church and admiring the new paint job, when I noticed what I thought was a slight lean in the 100-foot steeple. To confirm my suspicion, I hired a surveyor to plumb the steeple. Sure enough, it was leaning out from the church to the north about twelve inches off center.

I immediately called a meeting of my committee, where one of the older members said, "Oh, sure, it was leaning in 1938, but some of us shored it up. It's been that way ever since." The committee decided not to do anything.

Being an engineer, I thought more data might be helpful, so I asked the surveyor to come back in three months. This time, the steeple was leaning eighteen inches off center! The steeple now was downright dangerous. If it fell, it would fall into the front entrance where everybody congregated on Sunday morning after church.

But, I still couldn't get an agreement within the committee that we should replace the steeple.

I hired architects and engineers to look at it. They confirmed its poor condition, and expressed concern about safety. They also gave me an estimate of $180,000 to remove and replace it.

Now the problem was not just the stubbornness of the older New Englanders, but a financial problem for the congregation.

The situation was further complicated with the approach of autumn and the hurricane season. I was convinced that our beautiful, white, towering steeple would come crashing down. Yet, I still didn't have approval to spend the money, let alone destroy a historic structure.

A few weeks later, there was a forecast of high winds coming up the coast from a hurricane. I had about three days to do something. One of my committee members was an architect who shared my concern. He went to the New Canaan fire marshal, who looked over the situation; he *condemned* the church!

Fortunately the storm bypassed New Canaan, so we were allowed to use the church under certain limitations. I finally got approval to proceed with removing and restoring the church steeple. We brought in a helicopter and "decapitated" the church.

We had received the necessary approval from the New Canaan Historical Society to fix the steeple. Their only requirement was that the replacement had to be identical in design and construction to the old steeple.

After we removed the structure, which was over 100 years old, we found it had been constructed by shipbuilders. The center structure of the steeple was a huge, single-piece mast, around which the outside structure was attached. To our dismay, that building technique and skill no longer existed.

After an exhaustive search, including several trips to look at other churches where steeples had been replaced, we determined that the only solution was to replace our wood steeple with one made of *cast aluminum*! A company in Kentucky specialized in this product and guaranteed a perfect replica of the wood structure.

Imagine going to the New Canaan Historical Society with a proposal to use cast aluminum for our steeple! They reluctantly accepted the proposal and the job was done. It's beautiful, and looks exactly like the old one, except it doesn't lean.

I'm told that when people in New Canaan are asked if they know John Titsworth, they say, "Isn't he the one who had *THE* Congregational Church condemned?"

After a couple of years in venture capital, in 1985 I decided that maybe retirement wasn't a bad idea. I made a decision that I since have regretted often, and that was to sell the big house in New Canaan and move back to Minneapolis.

The house had tripled in value from the time we had bought it. This sale had seemed to be a good idea at the time, in view of a potential significant drop in my income. After all, when one retires, one is supposed to "sell the big house and move to a smaller place," isn't one?

If I could give advice to anyone thinking of retirement, I would say that if you are happy with your home, keep it. It doesn't matter if it is vacant in winter, if you like it, keep it! Living in a condo or townhouse with no yard, and someone else's trees and flowers, is for the birds.

As a matter of fact, full retirement is for the birds, also. We had bought a nice home in Florida in 1986, but after a year of golf, which I dearly love, I couldn't take it. I had to get back to a full-time job.

I knew that Don Massaro was looking for a CEO to run Priam Corporation, a disk drive company in San Jose. Don was the Chairman of the Board, but he was not active in the management of the company.

Priam was a public company whose stock value had fallen to $1.50 from $20, after a couple of years of poor performance. Joe Booker, from Shugart days, was President and CEO.

Don's feeling was that Joe couldn't make the tough decisions required of a turn-around situation, or might not have the vision to take the company forward into new product areas.

Actually, Joe was an excellent operating manager. Before I arrived on the scene, Joe had taken drastic action to reduce costs and generally restructure the company.

Don had called me in late 1987 and tried to get me to accept the presidency of Priam. I decided to give it a try, so in January, 1988, I called Don to tell him that I wanted the job.

I was hired as the President and CEO of Priam in February, 1988.

Before I took the job, Jeanette and I had lunch with Bill Hambrecht of Hambrecht and Quist, a large venture capital and investment banking firm in San Francisco.

Hambrecht and Quist had invested funds in a start-up company founded by Joe Booker. Joe's company had merged with Priam, so Hambrect and Quist subsequently owned a substantial amount of Priam common stock. Don Massaro, who had been on the Board of Joe's company, was on Priam's Board as a result of the merger.

At the luncheon, I told Bill that the problem at Priam was insufficient cash to develop new competitive products. The company was ten years old. Its initial products had done well, but the second generation of hard disk drives was late and of inferior design.

There was enough money being generated to bring out new designs, but I knew there was not enough cash to enter full production and introduce the new products to market.

Bill said to me something like, "If you can turn that company to profitability, I think we can find the necessary funding." I took that to mean that his firm would put up the money, probably by buying more equity or lending Priam the funds.

So, I started to work as CEO of Priam. In great part due to Joe Booker's previous actions, the company finished the quarter ending in July with a $4 million profit. I proceeded with the development of new products, knowing that we would be cash-limited in a few months, but assuming Hambrecht would come through with the necessary infusion of cash.

I wasn't depending merely on our luncheon conversation. Don Massaro, who was much better acquainted with Hambrecht than I, was convinced that we would get our funding.

I spent hours with Hambrecht's people, showing them what we were doing. I also showed them how our new products, including a 400 megabyte 3.5-inch drive, would surpass our competition and bring Priam back to being a viable and profitable company.

Therefore, Hambrecht and Quist certainly knew what we were doing. I must say, however, that Bill Hambrecht's subordinates, while attentive to my presentations, never really showed signs of confidence. I'm sure they influenced Hambrecht in his decision not to invest further in Priam.

That decision was made clear to me at another luncheon with Bill, shortly after our profitable quarter.

Tom Kamp, who had retired from Control Data, had agreed to do some consulting work for me and was on a visit to San Jose. I invited him to join Bill and me for lunch. After all, Tom was recognized as the most successful executive, ever, in the disk drive business. Tom was in complete agreement with my strategy, so I thought his support would be helpful with Hambrecht.

What a surprise I got at that luncheon! Bill Hambrecht spent almost the entire time lecturing me on proper techniques in management. He used as an example the management style of one of his associates who was the CEO at Mini-Scribe Corporation, a Colorado-based disk drive company somewhat bigger in size than Priam.

Bill said this manager's style in a turnaround situation like Priam or Mini-Scribe was to take the organization chart the night before arriving on the scene as the new boss, and put a red "X" through every other name. Then the manager's first action was to fire all the red "X's."

I wondered how he knew he was firing the right half, remembering my Bill Lear days.

Bill went on to say that the new manager would then set up quarterly incentives for the company executives who were left. These incentives were indeed rewarding, as well as intimidating, because if the targets were met, the executive got a bonus of 100 percent of salary. If the targets were not met, the executive got fired!

Bill further commented that he didn't like my style of management. He thought I should have approached the Priam job the way his man had done at Mini-Scribe. After all, Mini-Scribe was highly profitable, the stock was climbing astronomically, and all was well.

By contrast, I had given all of the top executives at Priam a *raise in pay*! (They hadn't had one for *years*. They were highly competent people, but they had lost confidence in themselves. I thought they needed a boost.)

Bill may have read articles on Priam and Mini-Scribe in an issue of a local technical magazine that had contrasted management styles. You may read the article about me in the Appendix. While Tom Kamp listened in amazement, Bill finished his lecture to me by saying that he had decided not to invest in Priam.

We were in real trouble! There was little time to cultivate new potential investors. Besides, no venture company or other financial institution would invest in Priam if one of the biggest shareholders (Hambrecht) wouldn't put up additional funds.

I had done some preliminary work in looking for a buyer of the company, and had talked to a number of investment bankers who thought we could get perhaps $4 per share for the company. I had also talked to Finis Connor about a merger, but Finis was afraid of the "baggage" represented by the old products at Priam; he was probably right.

Our only chance for survival was to sell the company to someone willing to put up $15 to $20 million in cash to bring out our new products.

In my opinion, the sale of the company could have been at almost any reasonable price, even at $1 per share. It was a $150 million company with potential to double its revenue in three or four years, with substantial profits. To me, a $40 million price for our 40 million shares certainly seemed reasonable for a potential buyer.

Without a buyer, the company would die within six months to a year.

These events occurred during the latter part of 1988. As luck would have it, my health became a problem. I noticed an occasional dizzy spell that fall, but thought I was just out of shape since I wasn't playing golf or getting exercise of any kind.

I got progressively worse, so I went to the Stanford Medical Center. There I met Dr. Henry Jones, who turned out to be one of the most competent physicians I've ever known. He quickly determined that I had become addicted to a form of Valium that for three years I had been taking as a sleeping aid.

This was something that should have been taken for only a few days. It had been prescribed to me following cancer surgery in 1985, but was so effective that I refilled the prescription continuously. Obviously, there had been a mistake at the pharmacy or misjudgment on the part of the prescribing physician.

Besides Dr. Jones' ability to diagnose my addiction, he turned out to be quite a counselor. I was deeply involved in Priam, was contemplating an offer to head a buyout of my old company, Control Data, and had just accepted the Chairmanship of my alma mater, the Rose-Hulman Institute of Technology.

Dr. Jones encouraged me to think about the real values in life, especially at my age of 64 years, like establishing lasting relationships with my children, grandchildren, and friends.

Here I was, ruining my health with the stress of managing a doomed company and considering a takeover fight for a $4 billion troubled company. Moreover, I was leading my college out of the Dark Ages of an all-male institution to co-education, against the wishes of a number of very influential Board members.

Boy, now *that's* dumb!

I told Jeanette that we were heading for Florida, where I was going to stay until I could recuperate from the addiction. I would appoint a new president of Priam and take over the Chairman's duties, which would be to sell the company. I cut off my association with the financial institutions which had pledged *$1.5 billion* of debt and $500 million of equity to buy CDC; that killed the deal.

I decided to remain as Chairman of my school, but to slow down the schedule for co-education. This was partly because I didn't have the energy to pursue it vigorously, and partly because we were splitting the Board. At that point, those problems were going to tear the school apart. I thought that a little more time would solve those difficulties, and I was correct.

I strongly recommended to the Board of Priam that we engage an investment banker to sell the company. I had already signed an agreement to do so, and we had conducted a preliminary search for such a buyer. All we had to do was finalize the agreement.

Don Massaro, who for all practical purposes represented Bill Hambrecht, convinced the Board that a sale of the company at such a low price was not the best way to go. Instead, the Board decided to bring in one of the boys with the red pen.

I resigned from Priam for health reasons, and watched the company go down the drain over the next several months.

I felt badly about this great little company. I really liked the people in its management and workforce. I would walk through the factories at least once a week and got to know everyone from the janitor to the engineers.

It's a shame the company went under, not only for the shareholders (of which I was one, having bought 150,000 shares at $1.50 per share when I joined the company), but even more so for the employees, who lost their jobs. A relatively small amount of cash could have given these people a very reasonable chance to succeed.

About the time I left Priam, rumors started coming out of Colorado about problems at Mini-Scribe. It seemed that my old associate, Dr. Bob Sparacino, had been brought in by the Board to head a committee to investigate certain irregularities.

It soon was discovered that management, apparently in fear of losing their jobs, had misrepresented income and profits. When they were short on shipments, they packaged *bricks* and shipped them to distributors, declaring them as disk drive revenue. Inventories were incorrectly recorded, and it was reported there was even an attempt to modify audit reports.

In short, the shareholders, stock market, and the Securities and Exchange Commission had been misled as to the performance of the company.

So much for the "red pen" and intimidation approach. In my opinion, this was related to two companies going down the tubes and a lot of jobs with them: Priam, because it didn't get needed financial support, and Mini-Scribe, because of very bad management practices.

The management style to which I am referring uses the kind of intimidation and pressure tactics that predictably drive some managers to cheat. This is not to say that there should be any excuse for such action, but people tend to do strange things when they are desperate.

All responsibility starts with top management. It is very unlikely that the Mini-Scribe situation would have occurred at Priam because people were treated with respect, and were positively motivated.

There is no substitute for honesty and fairness.

IX

REFLECTIONS

It is obvious in this book that I have been critical of large corporations. I have greatly oversimplified the situation.

Problems that arise in a company as large and successful as Xerox are not likely to be direct results of single decisions by individual managers. Problems come from early successes, high growth rates, and vast international interests. These elements go into building a culture and bureaucracy that are necessary to run a multi-billion-dollar, multinational business.

There is nothing wrong with bureaucracy itself, for it is a way to get complex things done. However, when people get complacent and allow the system to blindly run the business, then it becomes an obstruction to progress.

People get complacent when their business has become successful, especially in cases when the operation has been incredibly successful, such as Xerox. They fail to change the process of doing business so that it would adjust to new situations. They stop making decisions and thinking clearly; the whole system bogs down when the old culture is allowed to run a growing and changing business.

An organization's culture doesn't arise overnight. It took twenty years of success and almost uncontrollable growth (a few thousand people in 1960 to 120,000 people in 1980) for the "Xerox Culture" to become established.

Overall, it wasn't *bad*, either. No company had better industrial relations, better pay, better benefits, a better public image, or better shareholder relations than Xerox Corporation when I joined the company in 1979.

Personal integrity and honesty always have been among the strengths of the corporate leaders and officers at Xerox. This stems from the leadership of founder Joe Wilson and his subsequent CEO's: Peter McColough, David Kearns, and Paul Allaire.

The bad part of a corporate culture arises when dedication to it becomes too rigid, which then makes its operations inflexible. A huge business can become so complex that it begs for more human resources. One sign of this is big staff groups which try to rule by consensus, or worse, make decisions by procedure instead of thought.

Let me give you an illustration. A large corporation, which has been successful with its original product line, expands by acquiring a successful smaller company with a related but different product line. The smaller company becomes a subsidiary.

When the parent business falls on temporary hard times, it is reasonable to institute certain corrective measures: no overtime, a personnel cutback of 5 percent, lower annual pay raises or an extended period for pay raises, and no new hires. However, since we are *all* part of the corporation, these measures "must" apply across the board!

But, the subsidiary business has been booming. They need more salesmen, overtime to meet schedules, and generous raises to reward their entrepreneurial managers. No way! The "rule" always has been that everybody contributes!

The subsidiary management has to convince the parent company's staff to exclude them from the fiscal tightening. Such wrangles usually end up at the President's office. Sometimes, however, the subsidiary's management can't get through the bureaucratic maze to get to the President's office. These managers may end up making a token effort to comply, or find a way around the corporate directives, sometimes at great personal risk.

I've seen events like these occur more than once at CDC and Xerox. Strong subsidiary or division managers managed to avoid ruining their businesses through great additional efforts and negotiations with corporate staffs. Their time would have been better spent on attention to their own businesses.

Another example of rigid thinking is the situation where a large successful company acquires a smaller concern and decides to integrate the functions of the new company into its own functional organization. In other words, have the chief engineers in the acquired company report to the chief engineer of the parent company. The same would apply to the other departments, such as manufacturing, accounting, and sales.

Besides setting up cumbersome lines of communication, and stifling any semblance of flexibility and response to problem-solving, the new company is forced into the bureaucracy and "culture" of the parent.

It doesn't work! It can't work, and it is the road to disaster.

While every large company doesn't go to this extreme, most often try to impose too much of their bureaucracy and culture on their acquired organizations too soon. There is nothing wrong with gradually phasing in employee benefit programs, such as insurance benefits, pay policies, and vacation and holiday schedules. But, imposing specific methods for product development programs or applying corporate standards and policies indiscriminately across the board can demoralize and depress entrepreneurial spirit.

Most subsidiaries need to maintain their identity and they need to keep their leaders. Making a staffer from the parent company the head of a newly-acquired company is a paramount error.

What does one do to avoid the buildup of bureaucracy and "bad" cultural problems? Bill Norris had the right idea when he made a rule that no operation in CDC in a single location or division could exceed 1,000 people. He wanted smaller, more manageable, and highly responsive units in the company.

While we didn't generally stick to his "rule," it did result in a highly decentralized company. That was especially true in CDC's Peripheral Products businesses.

Tom Kamp, who was President of Peripheral Products, was very much an advocate of a decentralized organizational structure. He let his division presidents run their shows! Tom maintained a minimal corporate staff and encouraged entrepreneurial efforts. In fact, Tom was probably more entrepreneurial than most of his general managers.

This is not to say that the bottom line wasn't important! Tom insisted on performance; he didn't tell you how to get it, for that was up to you. He did allow all the freedom you needed. If higher corporate staff got in your way, Tom took care of that problem. He had the best leverage possible: a record of success with which no one could argue.

Later at CDC, with Bob Price, I had the same freedoms. We were masters of our own destiny. Of course, we were required to report our progress and problems, and had to submit budgets and long-range plans. If we didn't meet our budgets and plans, we had to have a good reason. If too many budgets were missed, there would be serious trouble, and reassignment was one solution.

The most critical goals for a high tech business is to stay current with the state of the art, and to see that the products are on the leading edge.

When I ran CDC's disk memory business, Lloyd Thorndyke was Vice President of Engineering, Gerry Gilbert was Vice President of Manufacturing, and Lee Kremer was our chief strategist. We always had a "new products" list planned for the next five years. We made sure that each engineering and research program was aimed at those products.

The same strategy was used when I headed computer systems. Norm Skinner and Bob Duncan scheduled and priced every upgrade in new technology for mainframes for several years into the future. *My rule was that every new product introduction or upgrade had to have a lower price to the customer and a higher profit margin to CDC!*

This meant that every price reduction had to result in a better profit margin for the company. This sounds impossible, but it wasn't. We introduced newer, better, *lower cost* technology with each new product!

I have no personal animosity against financial managers, in general. Chief financial officers, like Bill Fitzgerald at CDC and Walter Kirson at Xerox, had tremendous influence and control over the performance of my operations. They knew exactly why we were or were not successful, and they understood the need for product planning and development.

However, I have seen too many financially-oriented people get control of high tech corporations. Usually, they either lost sight of the need to foster innovation, or never understood it.

I also have seen tragedies where managers, even those who had technical backgrounds, are forced by the absolutely ridiculous pressures of Wall Street to pay too much attention to the short-term bottom line. Eventually, they ignore technical progress or kill it by "saving" money to bolster profits.

I have explained about how one might *avoid* bureaucracy and "bad" cultural traits. But what about the company that has not avoided bigness and has an entrenched culture?

In 1979, the management at Xerox, Peter McColough and David Kearns, could see that the bureaucracy and culture solidly in place was going to kill the company. Peter saw the need for Xerox to become something more than a copier company. He saw that computers and digital communications were the future.

This is why Peter had bought the Scientific Development System Corporation (SDS) in 1970.

Don Massaro once said that one of the smartest things Peter McColough did was to buy SDS, and another was to shut it down. Buying SDS gave Xerox the basic technology to later develop laser printers and other digital devices. Closing SDS got Xerox out of the mainframe business, in which IBM and very few others could succeed.

One could argue that Xerox paid too much for this digital knowledge. Nevertheless, Peter McColough, and later, David Kearns, were on the right track in trying to get into digital technology by buying businesses and starting up operations "outside" the copier empire.

I was hired to help Xerox get into the digital business by cleaning up faltering operations. My mission also was to introduce new products invented at PARC and integrate subsidiary products into the Xerox system product lines. Besides providing products for the Xerox systems business, the subsidiary companies were expected to be successful in their own right, through OEM sales to other corporations.

But there was more! By example, or perhaps osmosis, I think both Peter and David thought we could change the culture of Xerox.

This was an impossible task. How could an organization which was trying to achieve a business turnaround in most of its operations, and, at the same time, incurring the costs of new product introductions, possibly set any kind of example for the huge copier "money machine" organization?

No matter how well we introduced products, or how quickly and efficiently we designed new products, we couldn't show even modest profits early on. Our influence on the copier organization was zero.

Even corporate headquarters referred to us as the "non-copier" group! I was known as the "non-copier executive." Clearly my organization was not going to change the culture of Xerox.

One could argue instead that the Xerox culture had killed SDS, and later killed Shugart, Century Data, and Diablo as well.

The good news is that the Xerox bureaucratic culture was finally changed in the only way possible. To his great credit, David Kearns took hold of the giant copier organization and "laid down the law" for doing business in a responsive, quality-oriented, and customer-oriented way.

David set up smaller, manageable business units, eliminated most of the corporate staff, and established competitive benchmarking procedures. He introduced a Deming-like environment, where every employee in the company has a voice in how the company operates.

W. Edward Deming taught the Japanese how to incorporate into an organization a close relationship between the management and employees. Everyone works towards the best interests of the customer, which ends up being the same as the best interests of the company. More importantly, every employee knows his and the company's goals.

The result was that Xerox won the national Baldridge Award as a top quality-oriented, customer-sensitive and responsive company. The copier business returned to a good profit margin performance.

This example is one among many that shows that leadership makes the difference.

When corporate leaders become complacent or try to be everyone's friend, there is indecision or decision by consensus, which leads to the worst kind of bureaucracy. This occurs when no decisions are made, so that the bureaucratic process takes over.

When corporate leaders keep their organizations lean and make sure their people are doing what they do best, the company has a good chance to succeed.

The best example of this that I can give is Zytec Corporation, whose Board of Directors I joined when the company was founded in 1984. Zytec had been a small manufacturing unit of Control Data, and supplied the disk memory division with miniature power supplies.

Ron Schmidt, who had worked with me in my early CDC days, had bought the operation through a leveraged buyout.

In its early years, Zytec struggled to grow its power supply business, but considered entering some other business that would be a bit more "exciting."

My strong advice was: "Don't change your focus until you are the best power supply company in the world."

Ron Schmidt not only maintained the company's focus on power supplies, but more importantly, he was able to have Zytec embrace the Deming quality approach to running the business. In 1991, Zytec won the Baldridge Award, beating the largest corporations in the U.S.

I often have heard senior executives say that, "good management is good management." Essentially, they mean that if they are good at running a computer company, they would be good at running a finance company; after all, the same rules of good management apply.

To me, that's a lot of hogwash! Like the song in "The Music Man" says, "you've got to know the territory!"

One has to know enough about a business to keep from being cheated or misled. It is not enough to have someone else around who knows the business. If you are the boss, *you* are ultimately responsible. Therefore, don't get into a business you don't understand!

A first violinist may be a superb musical artist, but chances are that he won't play the tuba too well.

Too many corporate Directors are unfamiliar with the businesses on whose Boards they serve.

There is an argument that says that a company Board should contain at least one banker and a lawyer. I would have no problem with this if they understood the business. Otherwise, establish all banking and legal relationships through the corporate offices.

Directors are supposed to serve the shareholders. I do not believe that a Director who doesn't understand a business on whose Board he serves can represent the best interests of a shareholder.

I think too many U.S. corporation Board members are poor shareholder representatives. They seldom get involved enough to know what is going on. When there is real trouble, they worry about themselves more than the company or the shareholders.

I don't have a suggestion for a better system than the public corporation Board, but in my opinion, if every Director were knowledgeable about the business, then the investors would be better represented.

Something which disturbs me in the current trends of U.S. business is the push toward a service economy. Finance people in particular, including most of Wall Street, are in love with making money with money. Even if one can make an investment with no risk, this method of making profits for corporations (other than banks or insurance companies) does nothing for the long-term benefit of the company or the U.S. economy.

When companies like Xerox get into the insurance business, there is less emphasis on the development of new products. Add to that the fact that insurance is by no means a risk-free investment, as evidenced by the huge write-offs and losses during the last few years, this further erodes the companies' ability to invest in new technology.

The more our U.S. corporations tie up their money in service-oriented investments, the fewer products we will develop and the more dependent we will become on Japanese and other foreign manufacturers.

We seem to have forgotten that technology and new products have built the U.S. economy to its international leadership position. The lack of acknowledgement of the importance of technological leadership by the Federal government and the public in general, is beginning to show in our technical schools.

For example, enrollment in engineering colleges is declining. At the rate we are going, in ten years we will have more foreign students in U.S. engineering schools than students in those schools who are U.S. citizens.

We do not have the patience and understanding of the research and development process that we once have had. I saw this clearly when I was involved in the venture capital business.

Financial people in that business judge business performance only within very short periods of time. Venture capitalists talk about a ten-year maturity for their investment funds, but, believe me, if the fund does not look great in less than five years, the general partners have a tough time starting a second fund.

In a way, this leads back to the idea of "sticking to what you know and do best." A Board member should know the company's business and *support* it. Corporate management in high tech businesses should *stick* to high tech investments, whether these investments are acquisitions or internal research and development expenditures.

Either Wall Street should have the patience to look beyond quarterly results, or management should have the guts to ignore pressure from these short-term thinkers.

When I first started writing this book, I intended for it to be mostly humorous anecdotes from my business career.

While they may not have seemed funny at the time, looking back at episodes with Bill Lear now gives me a chuckle.

When I got to the Control Data and Xerox stories, I found myself getting more serious. I thought about telling "where the bodies are buried," but decided not to, even though that is what it would take to sell great quantities of this book to the general public. It is not my nature to tell stories "out of school," and besides, I don't care about selling a lot of books.

It is enough for me that my children and grandchildren will have a record of what their father and grandfather did in his business career.

Even with the trials and tribulations, I wouldn't want to change anything. I've had a great time, and made more friends than I can count. There's not a lot more that one can get out of life.

Last year, I was elected to be the Chairman of the Board of Managers for the Rose-Hulman Institute of Technology. Maybe Career Number Four is coming up!

APPENDIX

JOHN TITSWORTH, FROM FARM BOY TO CHAIRMAN

COMMUNIQUE MAGAZINE, FEBRUARY 1989

John Titsworth, a 20-year veteran in the industry, left his golf clubs behind to come out of retirement last year and take the reins of Priam Corporation as President and CEO. The company, based in San Jose, California, produces high performance, high capacity Winchester disk drives for the OEM and distributor markets.

Staff employees at Priam were in for a surprise when Titsworth arrived in February of last year. Instead of getting the ax, they got a raise and a strong dose of mid-American hospitality. Born and raised in Hutsonville, a farming community in southern Illinois, Titsworth worked quickly to instill the sense of pride and caring that is his heritage.

"I knew that the people here had gone through an awful lot of tough times," says Titsworth. "I wouldn't say that they were demoralized, but they certainly needed something to bolster company pride. So, my first target was to get the people here feeling good about themselves. You might ask, 'What does that have to do with business?' Well, I think it has everything to do with business."

Before he came on the scene, the company had already made some tough decisions to bring Priam back to profitability under the former President, Joe Booker. Cutbacks, layoffs and the decision to take some manufacturing offshore had wounded company morale. "This company was very proud of being a U.S. company and wanted to keep all the work here—they tried hard. They put in robots and that sort of thing, but they couldn't compete with all the other companies that went offshore. So, they finally had to make that decision," Titsworth explains.

With a little help from Old Glory, Titsworth began bolstering company self-esteem. Priam became the first building on the block to brandish the American flag. "Nobody around here has flagpoles up around their buildings. I wanted people to see the good old American flag up there flopping in the breeze when they came in. I thought maybe it would instill a little sense of pride." But there was more to Titsworth's plan than flag waving. Each week he ran around meeting employees in all levels of the company, shaking hands with everyone until he had personally met each worker.

Morale isn't the only thing that is improving at Priam. The company has posted a profit for four consecutive quarters now, with total revenues last year of $140 million. While Titsworth is reluctant to take credit for the company's recent profitability, his leadership is no doubt being felt. Before retiring, Titsworth served as Executive Vice President and Member of the Board at Xerox.

He was working for Control Data Corporation when Xerox discovered his talents. Under Titsworth's direction there, Control Data's failing mainframe business became the company's most profitable business. In seven years, he turned their nonexistent disk business into a billion dollar business. Small wonder he found himself bored with retirement and accepted Priam's offer.

Since coming to Priam, Titsworth's biggest challenge is one associated with the entire industry—how to keep up with the rapidly changing technology. "The disk memory business is the most technically difficult business in the industry, including all mainframes in the industry and all the PC's. It is the fastest changing technology, so it is the most difficult business to manage. Frankly, there are very few people who can manage a business like this in tough times. They're all good at managing it when it's booming, but as soon as there is a glitch, most people don't do very well," he says.

Pleased with the progress Priam has made so far, Titsworth sizes it up this way, "We don't make a lot of money, but we didn't lose $50 million either."

While Priam may be competing with bigger companies that have a lot more cash and, according to Titsworth, "spend it wildly," the company plans to outdistance its competitors. "If you follow this industry at all, you know that there are some very big companies that are in some very, very difficult trouble. But we keep chugging along," he adds with satisfaction.

Any respect Titsworth has won in the industry pales in comparison to the celebrity status he enjoys back in Robinson, Illinois, where Titsworth attended high school. In 1984, he was named "Distinguished Citizen of the Year." The folks around Robinson are proud of their "local boy who made good," and turned out by the hundreds to the banquet held in Titsworth's honor.

Titsworth himself seems to be the most surprised by the way things have turned out. As a young man growing up on a 60-acre farm during the Depression, he never dreamed he could afford college. "We were very poor. We had a nice family life but we didn't even have a car," he recalls with some amusement. In those days, Titsworth learned how to stretch a quarter (his weekly allowance). Entertainment meant hitching a ride into town for a 15-cent movie. "It really was a great time," he remembers.

Luckily, Titsworth was able to attend Rose-Hulman Institute of Technology in Indiana on the G.I. Bill, where he received his B.S. degree in Mechanical Engineering. He and his wife, Jeanette, and their first baby survived on a $105 a month for the three year period. "I weighed 129 lbs. when I came out of college. We actually went hungry at times," Titsworth recalls.

In spite of his lean beginnings, Titsworth has seen his share of glitz. After working for the Navy Department for a few years, he was taken under the wing of Bill Lear of Lear, Inc. Titsworth founded Jet Electronics and Technology Company, a subsidiary of Lear Jet, and went on to become Vice President of Lear Jet Industries in 1965. "We got more publicity than you can imagine in those days," he says with a sparkle.

In 1974, Titsworth received the Medal of Industrial Merit from the President of Portugal for establishing the first computer plant in that country. A more recent triumph for Titsworth was being elected to Chairman of the Board at Rose-Hulman, receiving an honorary doctoral degree from the institution he once thought he could never afford to attend.

Proud of his rural roots, Titsworth exudes a down-home charm that leaves him as comfortable in overalls as in a Lear Jet. "I go back to Illinois and put on my farm clothes just like everybody else," he says. "And, I'll tell you," he adds, "if you haven't been in the Saratoga Bar in Palestine, Illinois, you haven't been in rural America."

INDEX